Health-related fitness during pregnancy

by

Sylvia Baddeley

Quay
Books

Mark Allen
Publishing Ltd

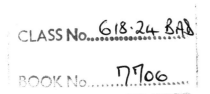
Quay Books, A Division of Mark Allen Publishing Limited
Jesses Farm, Snow Hill, Dinton, Nr Salisbury, Wiltshire, SP3 5HN

©Mark Allen Publishing Ltd 1999
ISBN 1 85642 130 9

British Library Cataloguing-in-Publication Data
A catalogue record for this book is available from the British Library

Printed in Great Britain by Redwood Books, Trowbridge, Wiltshire

Contents

Acknowledgements

Thompson and Floyd's 12th edition of *Manual of Structural Kinesiology*, published by Mosby, has been invaluable in helping to provide an excellent, comprehensive breakdown on how the body works during exercise. The physiological detail can be thoroughly recommended to any student or mother who wishes to delve more deeply into the analysis of exercise.

My thanks to Shân Green, whose expertise and enthusiasm has always encouraged me and to the Central YMCA based at Great Russell Street, London, who have been leaders in their field in developing appropriate training courses for midwives and exercise teachers specialising in ante- and postnatal exercise.

A special thanks to the thousands of women for their participation, enjoyment and appreciation over the last ten years in our exercise programmes. Their comments and support have been the catalyst that has forever changed the previous dichotomy between pregnant women and exercising. Both should lie as snugly together as a baby in the womb.

Introduction

The need for more information

Eight years participation in teaching classes and lecturing locally, nationally and internationally on exercise during pregnancy has highlighted a knowledge gap within the midwifery profession and the exercise world. A whole body and health-related fitness exercise programme is not available under one cover for the modern midwife or exercise teacher to use as a safe guide. Principles of fitness, exercise techniques and the intricacies of circuit training are readily available for the lay public and exercise trainers alike. Texts on preparation for labour and exercises during pregnancy are often described in layman terms (eg.'bottom kicks' instead of hamstring curls) and are not explicit enough for the professional in terms of how and why.

A book that covers kinesiology, the implications of pregnancy on exercise and general guidelines for everyday physical activity would act to consolidate the information given out at the many different types of workshop and short course that are now being offered to midwives throughout the UK. It would also embrace *Health of the Nation* initiatives on maternal health and allow the midwife to introduce systems of care that would help the pregnant woman adapt to her changing body dynamics. It will, hopefully, bridge the gap between training courses that have appropriate course content and those that do not and educate exercise teachers about the need for specialised classes for the pregnant woman.

This book is not intended to be a definitive work on exercise during pregnancy, but should be viewed as a stepping stone for all interested, teacher and student alike, in order that future generations of mothers will benefit and exercise will be viewed as a natural, enjoyable and very necessary part of antenatal education.

What is available at the present time

Antenatal exercise sessions are offered to pregnant women in a variety of ways by a number of different professional groups such as midwives, physiotherapists, swimming teachers and trained and untrained exercise instructors. Have these exercise sessions kept pace with the demands of fit, healthy pregnant women who wish to carry on exercising throughout their pregnancy and participate in jogging, circuit training, aerobics or step classes? Can they carry on? Are there contraindications? Who should be teaching them and is the research based information available at this present time being incorporated into advantageous exercise sessions that help them cope with the massive physiological adaptation that occurs throughout pregnancy and the postpartum period? This book presents an overview of what is currently on offer in the form of exercise sessions during pregnancy and attempts to find a way forward for the teacher and exerciser that would ensure uniformity of knowledge base, prevent conflicting advice and give an opportunity for interprofessional liaison and development in this area of expertise.

1

Background and national perspective

The word complementary is defined in the *Oxford Advanced Learner's Dictionary* as 'combining well to form a balanced whole'. Exercising our bodies at any stage of life viewed within this holistic context supports the theory of needing balance between mental, social, physical and medical well-being.

During my role as educator of the family unit, preparing families for the birth and subsequent care of their baby, I am also responsible for giving advice about changes in lifestyle and how to adapt to the massive physiological changes that are imposed on a woman's body throughout pregnancy and the early postnatal period. I have noticed how little the advice given to pregnant women on exercise had changed from the turn of the century. Berkeley (1920) stated that,

> ... the pregnant woman should lead as quiet a life as possible. She should have plenty of fresh air and take walking exercise daily, how far she should go varying with each individual, but at any rate it should be not far enough to cause fatigue. In addition, should the opportunity occur, she may motor or take carriage exercise; whilst if she is unequal to outdoor exercise then regular exercise in some other form which will strengthen the abdominal muscles should be taken. This may be done daily as follows; having divested herself of most of her clothing, she should lie on the floor, a rug intervening, and there with arms folded across the chest, raise herself into a sitting posture for several times in succession.

This description of an abdominal curl is viewed as controversial during pregnancy, although the concept of strengthening abdominal muscles is an admirable and up-to-date concept.

Certainly until the latter part of the 1980s exercises taught in parentcraft sessions throughout Great Britain consisted only of pelvic tilts (very valuable but contraindicated if taught lying flat on the floor — as they were and still are in places), knee rolling to work internal and external oblique muscles which form part of the abdominal corset (again taught flat on the back) and ankle rotations performed in order, presumably, to make the ankle joint mobile. I say presumably because the only input I and thousands of colleagues ever had during training was a two hour session with a physiotherapist who taught us how to teach 'breathing techniques for labour', pelvic tilts, knee rolling and how to improve posture throughout pregnancy. The emphasis was mainly on preparation for labour, not on how to adjust or adapt physical activity that took into account the limitations caused by the physiology of being pregnant.

Exercise adaptation as pregnancy progresses

The massive rise in interest in health-related fitness has posed questions for pregnant women and professional carers alike. Many young women of childbearing age are actively involved in contact sports (hockey, netball), participate in circuit training, using weights to work out different parts of the body on stationary work benches, or attend aerobics classes. The term 'aerobics' is misleading as it means with oxygen, and should be just part of a well-constructed fitness class that also includes a thorough warm-up session, components to work on muscular strength and endurance, a section on stretch to develop flexibility in order to minimise potential injury and a cool-down section at the end of the class. A woman may wish to carry on horse riding, continue with an advanced 'step class' or carry on cycling or jogging thirty miles a week. When pregnant women ask the question 'can I continue?' or motivated pregnant non-exercisers want to do something that is safe, but have never exercised before, how, professionally, should we advise them? What is safe, or controversial, and what has been researched?

The effects of pregnancy on exercise

How should exercise programmes be modified to ensure safety of the fetus and developing baby and why? In the first trimester (three months) of pregnancy one of the pregnancy hormones, relaxin, influences ligaments and supportive soft tissue. It softens them, thereby reducing stability of joints throughout the body. Obstetrically this is desirable as a little more 'give' within the joints of the pelvic girdle allows more room for manoeuvring when the baby enters the pelvic girdle, engages and settles into the delivery position, usually head down. The increase of body weight, increasing lordosis (extra curvature of the lumbar spine) and change in centre of gravity all produce more stress for joints around the body. Any exercise must take into account the increased dangers to joints, especially in the pelvic girdle and spine. There should be no impact during exercise regimes, no jumping up and down where the impact would be transmitted through the joints and the momentum of increased body mass would make it much more difficult to control direction and pace of movement. Relaxin hormone also affects the 'stretch' part of a fitness class. In exercise for non-pregnant participants, emphasis is placed on taking a joint beyond its normal range of movements in order to stretch the attached muscle. These manoeuvres promote flexibility around a joint and decrease the likelihood of injury during normal everyday activities, and in any particular sport. The unwary pregnant individual can exploit relaxin hormone effect and potentially destabilise joints even more. As ligaments have a poor blood supply it may be months before the ligament returns to its pre-stretched normal length and achieves joint stability once more. Although relaxin hormone is produced by the corpus luteum (on the ovary) from just two weeks gestation and then by the placental unit from 8–10 weeks gestation, the effects linger postnatally from 3–5 months in the body, even though the placental production unit was delivered after the baby. Therefore, postnatal classes should be structured with the effects of relaxin hormone in mind: that is minimal impact, maintenance stretch techniques and emphasis on pelvic floor exercise and abdominal work adaptations.

As pregnancy progresses, increased weight gain of three stone or more for the average pregnant woman, enlarging girth and continually adapting centre of gravity contribute to the pregnant woman becoming more clumsy and less coordinated. The rate and pace at which she moves and time given to changing direction are important considerations when planning an aerobic component performed to music and choreographed or planned by the exercise teacher. The American College of Obstetricians and Gynaecologists *Guidelines for Exercise During Pregnancy and Postpartum* state that maternal heartbeat should not exceed 140 beats per minute and that strenuous exercise activities should not exceed 15 minutes duration. Research suggests that there may be a shunt of blood away from the uterus and its contents in order to supply oxygen to larger muscle groups demanding more oxygen during aerobic work, for example the quadriceps or group of thigh muscles. Deep flexion or extension of joints should be avoided because of connective tissue or ligament laxity caused by relaxin. Also, all ballistic (jerky) movements should be avoided. No exercise should be performed in the supine position after the fourth month of pregnancy. Safety issues will be discussed in more detail in *Chapter 5*.

Benefits of exercising

What are the benefits of exercising the whole body in a structured, specific way rather than targeting just the pelvis or ankles or abdominal corset? In order to adapt to her changing shape and to help her cope with the demands of everyday living, a comprehensive exercise programme for the pregnant woman should include instruction on postural change and the how's and why's of achieving correct posture. Any muscle groups that will help her achieve this more successfully should be strengthened with appropriate exercises. For example, strengthening all the different muscle groups in the legs will help her to bend her knees, not her back, when bending and lifting. Using the strength of the quadriceps, hamstrings and gastrocnemius muscle groups will place less stress on her back and pelvis. Round shoulders are common in the pregnant woman, related to increase in breast size and weight and changes in centre of gravity. Shoulder retractions (contraction of trapezius muscle between shoulder blades) will not only help strengthen the upper back but also help to improve posture and stance. Aerobic work should be low impact, of about 15 minutes duration and should not raise the pulse rate higher than 140 beats per minute. This immediately creates a problem for most fitness teachers as their aerobic sessions or step classes are usually much longer than this. Aerobic work for the pregnant woman should be viewed as 'maintenance' work and not be pursued as an attempt to improve cardiovascular fitness, as you would normally expect for a class aimed at the general public. This dilemma poses the question of whether a pregnant woman is safe exercising in a class that is not specifically structured for the pregnant woman. The section of an exercise class that aims to improve muscular strength and endurance, aimed at 'working out' specific muscle groups around the body should be adapted accordingly, with particular attention being placed on body position, technique, number of repetitions (pregnant women tire more easily), alternatives and reducing workload as pregnancy progresses. Press-ups performed on the floor during the first trimester may need to be performed standing against a wall in the third trimester, or much sooner if carpal tunnel syndrome (tingling and numbness in hands and fingers) is present.

The benefits of exercise during pregnancy are now being recognised and highlighted by a number of researchers. The main objectives of ante- and postnatal exercise classes should be:

- to increase the pregnant woman's awareness and body control and help promote correct posture

- to maintain and promote circulation around the body. Specific exercises relating to pregnancy, such as pelvic floor contractions or exercising pectorals to help support increased breast tissue, should be incorporated into the exercise routines.

Attention should be paid to tailoring the intensity of exercise to different stages of ante- and postnatal work. A regular exercise programme two to three times per week specifically designed to take into account the limitations of pregnancy should help in maintaining mobility and teaching body awareness. Complaints about the minor ailments of pregnancy, such as varicose veins, haemorrhoids and morning sickness are reported less often by pregnant women who exercise regularly. These women also report improved sleep patterns, particularly within the third trimester. Any pregnant woman who attends any exercise class should be screened by the instructor before participation. Pertinent questions should include:

- have there been any problems in past pregnancies, in the present pregnancy or in conceiving?
- have there been any joint, muscle, bone, disc or back injuries?
- are there any medical conditions such as diabetes, epilepsy, heart disease or high blood pressure?
- are any medications being taken at present?

If the answer to any of these questions is yes, then a more detailed history should be elicited to ascertain if participation is advisable.

A typical structural outline of an exercise to music class, where the teacher plans or choreographs dance-like steps in between specific body movements would be as follows. The class would start with a 'warm-up' section. Major joints are mobilised and taken through a normal range of movement. Larger steps and body movements are introduced to slowly raise the pulse a little and improve blood flow to major muscle groups. The last part of the warm-up should be short-held static stretches to major muscle groups around the body, as pre-warmed stretched muscles contract and relax more efficiently. The warm-up is vital in all exercise classes as it reduces the risk of injury as well as preparing the body for the work that follows. The aerobic section of the class is aided by increasing pulse rates by using more dynamic, larger body movements which is achieved by working major muscle groups, such as the quadriceps and gluteals, in order to improve the efficiency of the cardiovascular system (heart and lungs). Following this, specific muscle groups around the body would be targeted and exercised. After the 'work' part of the class would be a 'cool-down' section where exercised muscle groups would be gently stretched to release tension within them, followed by a relaxation session at the end of the class. All parts of the class should be structured specifically to take into account the physiological changes induced by pregnancy and the limitations that they impose; specific training in ante- and postnatal exercise should be mandatory for the exercise teacher working in this area of expertise.

What type of antenatal exercise classes are currently available?

There are still many traditional parentcraft sessions being offered where exercises of a very limited nature are performed on the floor on a blanket. The exercising body is not viewed as a holistic unit; there is a fragmented approach, for example ankle twirling and pelvic floor exercises are still taught by many midwives in health centres or hospital centres. These classes are free. The National Childbirth Trust offers a planned programme of instruction and exercise, for a fee. This programme is taught in people's homes, usually on a rota basis, and the sessions are taught by their own extensively trained instructors. Emphasis seems to be placed on preparation for labour rather than a health-related fitness whole body approach.

A number of midwives around the country have attended post-basic training sessions on exercise during pregnancy. The length of courses varies from two to five days. Music is used as a motivator. The content and quality of these courses vary from area to area depending on the course leader's qualifications, expertise and experience in teaching people how to teach exercise, a very different concept from actually teaching an exercise class.

Because of their interest in health-related fitness a number of midwives have obtained the Exercise to Music Teacher's Certificate. Having obtained the knowledge and practical experience in teaching general public exercise, this training is followed by a further module on ante- and postnatal exercise. Practical and theory examination passes are needed to teach exercise to pregnant and postnatal women.

Leisure centres and swimming instructors are also becoming interested in offering water based exercise for the pregnant woman. Aquanatal exercise was introduced in Stoke on Trent in 1987 and has been enthusiastically used by many pregnant women. Many midwives have attended specific training events in order to offer aquanatal exercise to their pregnant clients. Once again, these courses vary in length, content and the expertise of the trainers. Water based exercise offers many advantages to the pregnant woman. The structure of the class is the same as land based exercise classes, but because there is less stress on joints exercise is possible for individuals with limited mobility. The haemo-dynamic changes of pregnancy affected by immersing oneself in water may put less strain on uterine blood flow than land based exercise, and the 'resistance' factor of water enhances the effects of exercise. Chronic backache is often relieved as the weight of the uterus and its contents are temporarily suspended during immersion. Women feel lighter and more graceful, leading to improved self-esteem.

Contraindications for exercise

The exercise teacher should evaluate, through the screening process, each individual who wishes to exercise during pregnancy. The following conditions may contraindicate vigorous physical activity. These are taken from the American College of Obstetricians and Gynaecologists Guidelines:

- high blood pressure
- anaemia or other blood disorders
- thyroid disease
- diabetes
- cardiac arrhythmia or palpitations
- history of precipitous labour
- intrauterine growth retardation (smaller growth than expected during pregnancy)
- bleeding during pregnancy
- breech presentation during the last three months of pregnancy

- obesity
- extreme underweight
- history of three or more spontaneous miscarriages
- ruptured membranes ('waters' broken or draining)
- history of premature labour
- diagnosed multiple pregnancy (twins, triplets)
- incompetent cervix or neck of womb
- diagnosis of placenta praevia
- diagnosis of cardiac disease.

Any of the following symptoms and signs should warn the woman to stop exercising and seek advice from her midwife or doctor:

- pain
- faintness
- bleeding
- rapid pulse on resting
- dizziness
- back pain
- shortness of breath
- pubic pain
- palpitations
- difficulty in walking.

Further benefits

There are inherent benefits in exercising during pregnancy in terms of maintaining muscle tone, building strength and endurance, and protecting against back pain. Positive effects are noted in the improvement of mood and self-image. In the postpartum or post-delivery period potential back pain and injury remain a significant problem for many women, as the daily care of a young infant involves repeated bending, lifting and carrying. Of great benefit would be an exercise programme that incorporated back, leg and abdominal strengthening exercises as well as utilising the pelvic tilt and pelvic floor exercises.

The way that we, as professionals, introduce and offer antenatal and postnatal exercise programmes may have far-reaching consequences that will influence the uptake or rejection of such services. Midwives and other professionals have a unique opportunity to influence and improve the health of the nation. Privileged and prolonged contact with the family unit places them in a position to influence attitudes on healthy lifestyles.

This should be a prime objective, both on an individual professional basis and at a national level.

Six years involvement in teaching practical exercise classes to pregnant women, as well as being involved in developing and offering training modules to midwives and exercise teachers, has placed me in a privileged position that has allowed me to gain a national overview of the development of the antenatal exercise to music service within the UK. Many conversations with midwives, students, trained and untrained exercise teachers and leisure service managers have prompted me to ask a number of questions.

Who should be/who is teaching pregnant women to exercise?

Immediate and obvious choices are midwives, physiotherapists and fully trained exercise instructors who have completed a specialist module of training on antenatal and postnatal exercise. Other groups are also showing interest, such as health visitors who are keen to initiate postnatal support groups and exercise classes. Swimming instructors, who have various training courses, are showing interest in a variety of leisure centres about the country. Physiotherapists and midwives with varying levels of expertise and practice in health-related fitness are teaching practical classes to the pregnant population. Trained and untrained exercise instructors are also teaching exercise to music classes, some in partnership with a midwife, some not.

Who should be teaching pregnant women to exercise? Is any one group or profession better equipped than another? Could any one specific group care adequately for the whole of our pregnant population assuming that rising levels of interest continue.

Is there any standardisation of training course content? The short answer to this, at the moment, seems to be a resounding no. Courses vary from half a day in length to three to five days, with a huge variety of presentation and omission of what should be a very structured base on which to build competence. If the professional wished to offer an antenatal or postnatal exercise to music session, land or water based, there should be an agreed modular structure that incorporates knowledge on health-related fitness principles, structure of a fitness class, understanding principles of warm-up, cardiovascular work, muscular strength and endurance and stretch principles and implications. Knowledge of how muscles work and the body interacts during exercise is vital. Teaching position, technique, correction points, alternatives and contraindications must form a major part of the training module. The physiological limitations that pregnancy imposes on exercises and the importance of screening are all vital ingredients of any introductory course encompassing exercise and the pregnant woman.

Motivated midwives and professionals are eagerly grasping training initiatives. Midwifery managers want to develop these sessions for their community sector or hospital bases. NHS Trusts are aware that offering specially designed exercise classes for pregnant women may increase the use of their services.

The diversity of courses and their contents could lead to a fragmented, inadequate uncoordinated service, with varying degrees of competencies and knowledge. The exercise world boasts some excellent training organisations (London Central YMCA at the forefront) and some training courses incorporate a 'taster' session on the complexities of pregnancy and exercise that attempts to introduce the subject into their 100 hour teacher training course in order to convince potential exercise teachers that antenatal exercise is a specialist area that needs very specific training.

There seems to be no defined professional who is responsible for teaching ante- and early postnatal exercise. At present midwives, physiotherapists, exercise teachers, swimming teachers, leisure centre employees and individuals not holding a nationally recognised teaching certificate are all involved in different ways in teaching pregnant and postnatal women. The lack of any national structure seems to inhibit the incorporation of such fundamentally important principles of health-related fitness into the minds of midwives, other professionals and mothers.

2

Physiological adaptations that affect exercise

The physiological adaptations of pregnancy result in major changes in every system of the body; pregnancy influences a woman's ability to exercise. By being aware of these changes and how they affect exercise performance, the exercise instructor should be able to adapt or prepare an exercise programme that will take these changes into account, enabling the development of a safe, effective exercise programme.

Muscular skeletal changes

The uterus, a muscular bag containing the growing baby, is one of the main causes of the dynamic changes in posture and gait during pregnancy. Normally a pelvic organ, after twelve weeks gestation the uterus with its expanding contents becomes an abdominal organ that presses forwards on to the abdominal corset, producing a characteristic waddling gait, and exaggerated lordosis (increased curvature of lumbar vertebrae) in the lower spine.As the uterus grows bigger, its dimensions at term increase 1500 fold. It weighs up to 20 times more and, counting its contents, is responsible for around 6kg of maternal weight gain.

This anterior or forward displacement of the uterus results in a change in the pregnant woman's centre of gravity, creating increasing lordosis as pregnancy progresses. Rotation of the pelvis on the femur (long thigh bone), contributes to the centre of gravity moving backwards, preventing the woman toppling forward (see *Figure 2.1*). Stability is maintained at the expense of a greatly increase workload on the spine, as the uterus, or womb, rotates to the right. As it increases in size, the uterus, creates a high, unstable centre of gravity that will affect a woman's balance and movement control. Because of these changes any exercise programme must consider a pregnant woman's inability to change direction quickly and safely. Any weight transference and pace of movement should allow her time to move with control, in order to minimise uncontrolled momentum, poor quality exercise technique and an increased risk of injury.

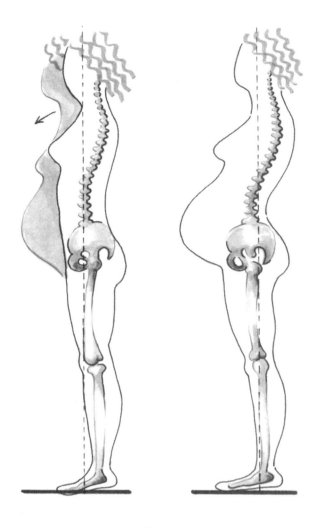

Figure 2.1

When beginning to exercise consider:

- starting position
- balance
- weight transference
- change of direction
- speed of movement
- movement control
- exercise technique.

When planning any exercise regimes for pregnant women, reaction time combined with rapid movement and change in balance has safety implications.

Relaxin hormone

This is produced from two weeks gestation by the corpus luteum, on the ovary, reaching its peak level at just twelve weeks gestation and is maintained until full term. Although this hormone and other pregnancy hormones, especially progesterone, also affect ligaments and supportive tissue and are excreted and back to pre-pregnancy levels by thirty days postpartum, the effects on ligaments and soft tissues may be evident for three to five months following delivery. This will mean that the precautions taken during pregnancy because of relaxin and progesterone influence should be continued for three to five months postnatally, low or non-impact movements, maintenance stretch only, not developmental.

Relaxin hormone does what its name suggests: it relaxes ligaments and connective tissues. Obstetrically, this is desirable, producing a little more 'give' especially with the pelvic girdle where available space is at a minimum in the last few weeks of pregnancy. Because ligaments throughout the body are affected and softened, stability of joints may be reduced in all parts of the body. Areas at great risk are the spine and the pelvis. The increasing workload on both of these areas, caused by the weight of the pregnant uterus, emphasises the need for caution, minimising exaggerated movements, twisting, or uneven weight distribution on these areas of the body.

Although increased relaxation of ligaments occurs throughout pregnancy, the last three months may show reduced mobility of the wrist and ankle joints caused by internal oedema (swelling) in connective tissues in these areas of the body. Visible ankle oedema is common in many women during the later stages of pregnancy, but it must not be assumed that this is physiological oedema caused by the normal haemodynamic changes of pregnancy. Hypertensive disease of pregnancy or pregnancy induced hypertension may be a pathological cause of oedema that has serious consequences for the mother and baby. A professional opinion from a doctor or midwife must be obtained by the exercise teacher before allowing participation. Any sports that require manipulative skills of ankles or feet and agility, strength and balance can potentially be more injurious to the pregnant woman, especially after the first three months of pregnancy. Therefore skiing, tennis, horse riding and gymnastics should be avoided. Swimming is not a threat and can be continued.

The respiratory system

Extensive changes occur early on in pregnancy due to hormone influence, especially that of progesterone. The diaphragm rises 4 cm, caused by the flaring of the lower ribs, increasing the transverse diameter of the lower ribcage giving more room for the expanding uterus (see *Figure 2.2*.) The medulla in the brain

becomes more sensitive to carbon dioxide. Increased ventilation is achieved by the pregnant woman breathing more deeply, not more often. Increased sensitivity to carbon dioxide should dictate appropriate aerobic workloads that will not be detrimental to the mother and therefore the fetus or baby. The maternal increase in oxygen consumption (20%) is adequately compensated for by the 40–50% increase in ventilation of the lungs, a factor that may be the cause of increased breathlessness during pregnancy.

The cardiovascular system

Cardiac output (amount of blood pumped out by the heart) increases by 40% during pregnancy and blood volume increases by 50%, created by a 50% increase in plasma volume and a 20% increase in red cell volume. Although a dilution effect of the

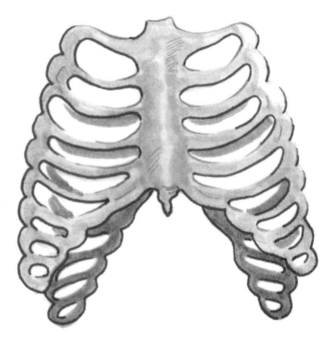

Figure 2.2: The darker shading showing the original position of the ribcage prior to pregnancy

ratio of red cells to plasma appears to take place, this relative reduction does not interfere with oxygen distribution to various organs. The major increase in cardiac output occurs at the end of the first three months of pregnancy, when oxygen consumption begins to rise.Increases in blood volume and cardiac output both peak towards the end of the sixth month of pregnancy. Resting heart rate begins to rise as early as the eighth week of pregnancy by eight beats per minute. By 32 weeks gestation the resting heart rate may be 20 beats higher than when non-pregnant (see *Figure 2.3*). To achieve this, the heart grows bigger and stronger. The contractility of the heart muscle also changes during pregnancy.

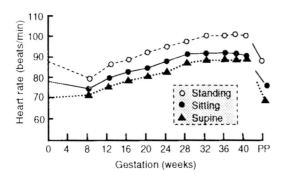

Figure 2.3

Whether increased or decreased activity takes place is still a subject of much debate. Mean arterial pressure drops resulting in a lowered blood pressure at around 20 weeks gestation and slowly rises to normal values at term.

These changes will have a great bearing on aerobic work. The rate and pace and length of time that it is considered safe for a pregnant woman to work will be influenced by these factors. A raised resting pulse rate will dictate that the 'warm-up' and preparation of the body prior to exercise may need to be shorter as body temperature is also raised during pregnancy. A warm-up component consisting of joint mobilisers, pulse raising and short held stretches should also take into account that the subsequent aerobic work should not raise maternal pulse above 140 beats per minute (American College of Obstetricians and Gynaecologists guidelines for exercise during pregnancy). Precise planning and structuring of the workload during warm-up and aerobic work should ensure that these safety guidelines are not exceeded.

Physiological anaemia takes place during pregnancy and is a natural response to the dilution effect of the 50% increase in plasma volume (the watery content of blood) and a smaller increase in red cell volume. Physiologically, this 'thinning out' of the blood helps perfusion of blood flow through the placenta (or afterbirth) to be achieved more easily. If the pregnant woman has a low haemoglobin level (below 10gm) early in a pregnancy, this dilution effect usually drops the level further causing increased breathlessness, fatigue and a decreased tolerance towards aerobic work. Regular screening is vital to ensure a safe aerobic workload at all times throughout pregnancy.

How relaxin hormone affects exercise during pregnancy.

1. Relaxation of ligaments and connective tissue throughout the body increases the risk of unstable joints from five weeks of gestation onward, and for three to five months postnatally. Areas of the body particularly at risk include the spine, the pelvic girdle and weight bearing joints such as hips, knees, ankles and vertebrae (especially in the lumbar region of the spine).

2. Relaxin hormone increases an individual's capacity for flexibility, allowing stretching of muscle fibre to be performed in positions that take joints beyond a normal range of movement. As the stretch increases, relaxin affects ligaments allowing more movement to take place, potentially placing more stress on the joint. For this reason, care should be taken when performing stretch routines during the end of the 'warm-up' component and during the 'cool-down' part of the exercise class. Short held stretches (8–10 seconds) with no bouncing or ballistic jerky movement for that individual will considerably lessen the risk of destabilising joints.

3. Joints in the pelvic girdle which are particularly affected by relaxin include the hip joints and the symphysis pubis joint at the front of the pelvis and both sacro-iliac joints situated on the

back wall of the pelvis. These can be seen externally just above the gluteal cleft, just below the lumbar region of the spine, by the presence of the sacral dimples. As the weight of the pregnant uterus increases, more stress is placed on these joints. Uneven pressure on the pelvic girdle will place more stress on particular joints in the pelvis. Prolonged standing on one leg (such as when performing side leg raises) throwing out a hip on to one side with a toddler held on the other hip, and standing using poor posture technique will all create uneven pressure and increase the risk of back pain and discomfort.

The symphysis pubis joint at the front of the pelvis has a gap of 4mm that increases to 9mm throughout pregnancy. Obstetrically this is desirable, increasing the pelvic outlet and facilitating delivery. Pain in this area may be a warning sign of increasing mobility in this joint and a less stable pelvic girdle. Wide side stepping movements should be avoided, or any move that involves increased 'pull' on this joint. If the abductor muscle group is being exercised, eg. side leg lifts, ensure that the lift is not too high to the side as a muscle group is attached to the symphysis pubic joint and will increase tension of pull on the joint as the leg is lifted out to the side.

Effects of exercise on maternal and fetal well-being

The cardiovascular system (heart and lungs)

1. **Cardiac output:** When exercising during pregnancy this is greater even at the same work-load. This augmented output helps to maintain uterus and fetus. A lower atrial ventricular differentiation suggests that higher cardiac output is distributed to a non-exercising vascular bed (the fetus or baby), so the body compensates for its specific needs during pregnancy.

2. **Uterine blood flow:** Recent work suggests no change in human placental blood flow (in the upright position) working at mild/moderate levels of exercise. The reduction in blood flow is related to severity of exercise. The uterine blood flow is potentially reduced as muscle groups demand a greater flow of blood to oxygenate them.

3. **Vulnerable times for the fetus or baby:** The first six weeks of fetal life in the regular exerciser who pushes her core body temperature above $40^{\circ}C$. Research in animals shows that a teratogenic effect (abnormal development of some organs or systems) can be created if the maternal core body temperature is raised above normal levels, as can happen if working aerobically for long periods.

4. **Metabolism:** The normal pregnant state gives some insulin resistance hence, 'the diabetogenic state of pregnancy', Type 1 diabetics should probably not exercise. Type 2 become more sensitive to insulin in pregnancy (if exercising) and may have reduced need for insulin then. Specialist advice from the consultant, midwife and GP should be obtained before exercising.

5. **Beta endorphin response during exercise**: Resting beta endorphin levels are increased during pregnancy. Levels are higher at the beginning of pregnancy and decrease in the second trimester. During exercise, beta endorphin levels rise as a direct response to increased physical activity.

6. **Oestrogen is an anabolic hormone:** Women athletes on the pill may perform better.

7. **Hypervolaemia of pregnancy results in 1 litre of extra blood during pregnancy:** Hypervolaemia means increase in volume, and during pregnancy the amount of blood in circulation is increased by 40–50%. It is interesting to note that athletes who participate in endurance training also increase their blood volume. The cardiac output is also increased, the heart enlarging during pregnancy to cope with the increased demands. Because the fetus produces carbon dioxide as a waste product, the pregnant woman needs a more efficient system of removing waste products. Her body responds by becoming more carbon dioxide sensitive. The increased feeling of breathlessness reported by many pregnant women is attributed to this. The pregnant woman responds by utilising a natural physiological hyperventilation. (For more information read the study, 'The effect of participation in regular exercise programme upon aerobic capacity during pregnancy' by Southpaul, Rajagopal and Tenholder, *Exercise in Pregnancy* **71**(2): Feb 1988).

Effects of exercise on the fetus

Oxygen extraction

In utero the fetus is permanently at 'high altitude' (20,000 feet).

1. The fetus copes with its intrauterine high altitude by raised haemoglobin levels (up by 50% in utero).

2. O_2 is 'bound' more efficiently to the red cell in the fetus. At birth fetal haemoglobin accounts for 80% of red cells; by four months of age, only 10% of fetal haemoglobin remains in the baby's blood (erythrocytes live only 120 days).

Fetal heart rate

This gradually increases throughout exercise. Ideally, exercise for 15–20 minutes, then rest, then a little more exercise and so on (see 'changes in fetal heart rate').

How exercise affects the fetus

Women who wish to carry on exercising throughout their pregnancy need to be aware of potential hazards to the fetus. Health clubs, gyms and exercise instructors should alert their pregnant clients to problems that could occur in order to minimise the risks.

Excessive heat production

Several research projects with animals and humans highlight the fact that intensive exercise that raises the maternal core body temperature to 39°C or above for 15 minutes or more may cause fetal abnormality. This link between hyperthermia (high temperature) and congenital malformation appears to be well established in experimental animals. A higher incidence of neural tube defects (eg. spina bifida) has been demonstrated in animals, although the association in humans is less certain.

Dehydration

Intensive exercise for 15 minutes or more (eg. intermediate or advanced classes with 30 minutes or more of aerobic work or step classes) may lead to dehydration. This in turn can precipitate premature labour and the risks that involves, ie. low birth weight, infection, respiratory immaturity etc.

Changes in fetal heart rate

One of the body's responses to intensive exercise is the production of catcholamines. Normally only 10–15% of these cross the placenta or afterbirth and reach the fetus. They can cause vasoconstriction (narrowing of blood vessels) reducing blood flow to the uterus and its contents, potentially causing low oxygen levels and fetal asphyxia. This theorising is more than a possibility, although some studies have suggested that a drop in the fetal heart rate (as well as a rise from the normal baseline) may be a normal response to exercise.

The usual response of the fetus to exercise is a corresponding rise in fetal heart rate of between 10– 30 extra beats per minute, irrespective of weeks gestation or intensity of exercise. Most fetal heart rates in women who exercise at mild or moderate intensity return to their normal baseline within 15 minutes of stopping exercise, but women who workout intensively will have fetal heart rates that take 30 minutes or more to return to normal baseline rates.

Reduction of blood flow to the uterus or womb

A potential problem of an intensive workload is reduced blood flow to the uterus or womb, as the larger muscle groups such as the thighs or quadriceps, demand more oxygen during aerobic work. This problem accompanied by elevated catecholamine levels can lead to brief periods of fetal tachycardia that are generally well tolerated by the fetus, demonstrated by a rising fetal heart rate while exercising. Prolonged hypoxia (low oxygen levels) may result in bradycardia (lower than normal fetal heart rates). Fetal bradycardia is a fairly rare event and usually indicates fetal distress.

These areas of concern can be dramatically reduced and an optimal safer environment for the fetus maintained by following specific guidelines.

3

Postural adaptations during pregnancy

Backache during pregnancy is accepted as the inevitable consequence of advancing gestation and childbearing. Many midwives also resign themselves to inevitable complaints from their pregnant clients and feel that there is little that can be done that will substantially alleviate back pain.

Posture adjustment when carrying a fetus in the anterior pelvic region has been observed to produce an anterior tilt of the pelvis, an increase in kyphosis and modifications in lordosis. Recent quantitative investigations, however, suggest that a variety of posture adjustment strategies are used to compensate for the anteriorly applied load during pregnancy.

Pregnant women may adjust their posture to maintain stability either by increasing or by decreasing the lumbar curve. Moore *et al* (1988) propose that flattening of the lumbar spine may be due to reduced iliopsoas (hip flexor) muscle activity. As the fetal mass (baby) positioned anterior to the hip joint axis grows, the flexion torque created by this weight will also increase. Thus, the flexion torque created by the iliopsoas is no longer needed. The addition of mass associated with the fetus may also be counterbalanced by a compensatory shift of the mass of the upper trunk. This posterior or backward shift of upper body mass is evident in those demonstrating an increase in lumbar curvature. NB: Torque — a force which produces rotation.

A better knowledge base of the physiology of backache during pregnancy can only enhance professional strategies for coping with this common complaint and play a positive role in holistic health issues, not just during the childbearing years.

Pain in the lower back region may also be reduced by improving the strength and control of the muscles attached to the spine and pelvis. Increased pelvic tilt may be reduced by activating the abdominal and hamstring muscle groups and by relaxing and/or stretching of the erector spinae and hip flexors. When activated (contracted) the hamstrings and the abdominal muscles produce forces that create an internal torque, (rotational force) opposing the torque created by the mass positioned anterior or the joint axis. During advanced stages of pregnancy, the abdominal muscles are lengthened, which reduces their effectiveness in reducing anterior pelvic tilt. In this case, the hamstrings must produce additional force to compensate for the reduction the in force supplied by the abdominal muscles. Those patients experiencing low back pain originating from increased anterior pelvic tilt may find relief by increasing the strength of the hamstring muscles and using them to reduce the increased anterior tilt of the pelvis. Similarly, low back pain originating from posterior pelvic tilt may be relieved by activating the erector spinae and hip flexors and stretching the hamstrings and abdominals. Flexibility exercises should be used with great caution by pregnant women; laxity of the ligaments and joints may be significantly altered by hormonal changes associated with pregnancy (see *Figure 3.1*).

Figure 3.1

Effects of pregnancy on the spinal column

1. The natural curves of the spine become more pronounced because of:
    i.   increased body weight
    ii. the centre of gravity moving forward
    iii. increased lordosis (curvature of lower spine).

2. Increased stress to the spine causes the pelvis to tip forward (anterior pelvic tilt) resulting in:
    i.   poor posture
    ii. backache
    iii. fatigue.

3. Insufficient support from the abdominal corset may be present because of:
    i.   poor tone before pregnancy
    ii. pendulous abdomen caused by frequent pregnancies
    iii. separation of the rectus abdominis.

4. Dynamic skeletal changes caused mainly by the 6kg of extra weight in and around the uterus producing a massive extra workload for the spine.

5. The forward tilt of the uterus into the abdominal cavity produces increasing lordosis.

6. The body compensating as the pelvis rotates on the head of the femur, moving the centre of gravity back over the pelvis in order to preventing toppling forward.

7. Increased forward flexion of the cervical spine, slumping abduction of the shoulders, leading to pressure on the ulnar and median nerves producing a carpal tunnel syndrome.

8. The enlarging uterus rotating on its long axis to the right resulting in instability and uneven distribution of the 'pregnancy load'.

9. Increased weight of breast tissue (up to 500g) affecting the centre of gravity.

Implications of relaxin hormone

1. Relaxin effects are present throughout the body.
2. Relaxin produced by the corpus luteum from two weeks gestation reaching and maintaining highest levels from 12 weeks gestation until term.
3. Although most hormone levels are almost back to normal 30 days postpartum, relaxin effect lasts for three to five months postnatally.

Relaxin hormone is present in the body before pregnancy occurs and is increased tenfold throughout the gestation period. Its effect is to aid relaxation of joints throughout the body, especially within the pelvic region. Other hormones are probably also responsible for this effect, such as progestogens and cortisols. At two weeks gestation, the corpus luteum on the ovary begins to produce relaxin hormone and its levels rise to reach a peak at 12 weeks gestation. This is maintained until term. Following delivery, levels begin to drop but the effects of relaxin hormone on joints in the body will be present in varying degrees for three to five months postnatally.

Effects of relaxin hormone

Relaxin hormone affects ligaments and connective tissue by softening them. As ligaments play an important role in stabilising joints, the reduction in ability to keep a joint firmly in place will affect to a great degree what and how much exercise can be performed safely in pregnancy and the postpartum period. Technique, rate and pace of movement and body position will all place demands upon less stable joints. When planning a programme of exercise, the teacher must take these factors into account in order to ensure that safety is not compromised. All midwives and many pregnant women are aware of joint changes that take place within the pelvic region, such as changing posture, separation of the symphysis pubis joint and the inevitable ensuing backache. These changes have wide implications for the planning, teaching and adaptation of any exercise session that is aimed at pregnant or postnatal women. The pelvic region is especially at risk as the weight of the uterus increases. The symphysis pubis joint, the two hip joints and both sacro-iliac joints on the back wall of the pelvis will all be affected and destabilised by the effects of relaxin hormone. These effects are examined in *Chapter 7*, where exercises and teaching points to minimise risk are discussed.

All aspects of a fitness class will be affected by the effects of relaxin hormone, especially the stretch components and the muscular strength section. While it should be remembered that the extra 'give' around joints may be obstetrically desirable during pregnancy, it is vital that exercise teachers and participants do not use the extra range of movement that pregnancy bestows.

The effects of postural adaptation during pregnancy

1. Changes in the centre of gravity cause increased weight to be thrown back on to the heels.
2. The head and shoulders may poke forward increasing curvature of the cervical spine.
3. The workload for the spine increases as it tries to compensate causing backache.
4. High heeled shoes, if worn, throw the body weight forward causing increased lumbar curve and strained ligaments in hips and knees.

5. The extra weight thrown forward into the toes causes stress to the arches and balls of the feet.

6. Continued wearing of high heeled shoes causes shortening of gastrocnemius muscles and discomfort when later flatter shoes are adopted as the muscle will be stretched.

7. Prolonged forward tilt of the pelvis causes the rectus abdominis to stretch and lengthen. Separation of the rectus abdominis reduces support to the lower back. Muscles surrounding the lower back shorten and become tighter, further increasing and adding to lordosis.

8. The centre of stress for all these dynamic changes in the spine is where the spine joins the pelvis, that is the most common region for backache, the lumbar region.

Maintaining correct posture during pregnancy

Exercises to improve posture include:

*   **Half squats and squatting**: to help strengthen leg muscles and aid correct bending and lifting techniques.

*   **Static abdominal contraction**: before 16 weeks gestation, abdominal curls can be performed. After this time static abdominal contraction will help maintain some tone in the abdominal corset which will have the secondary effect of helping to support the lumbar region of the spine.

*   **Hamstring curls**: these will help maintain the correct alignment of the pelvis and spine when the rectus abdominis stretches in the third trimester and produces inadequate torque forces to maintain the anterior pelvic tilt.

*   **Trapezius squeezes**: exercising muscles groups in the back will help maintain correct posture and thus help reduce backache.

*   **Latissimus pulls**: exercising the latissimus dorsi muscle group will also aid posture and improve lifting techniques, helping to protect the spine further.

*   **Gluteal contractions**: contracting the buttock muscles will improve muscle tone and help correct bending and lifting techniques, reducing stress on the spine.

Squatting

Squatting with a straight back develops good balance which protects the back from injury when lifting. Regurgitation of acid contents of the stomach can be prevented by this method. To maintain a squatting position, the body weight has to be supported by:

*   hyperflexed knees
*   hyperflexed hips
*   flatly positioned feet
*   flexibility around Achilles tendons
*   dorsiflexed ankles.

Many women cannot achieve this whether pregnant or not. Practice of the squat position before conception and throughout pregnancy would be required for the woman who wishes to squat for prolonged periods during labour and delivery. Squatting increases the diameter of the pelvic outlet and can be used during the second stage of labour to facilitate delivery. Ideally, the midwife, the woman and her partner should have a sound knowledge of bending, lifting and squatting techniques.

Correct bending and lifting techniques

Training of the pregnant woman in correct bending and lifting techniques can do much to reduce stress to the back and help her to cope with everyday activities around the home and family. Some points of consideration include:

- bend the knees, not the back
- keep the weight being lifted close to the body
- use one hand and a support if possible
- use the strength in the quadriceps (thighs) and gluteal muscle, to push upright keeping the back straight.

The incorrect positions are illustrated below by figures A and B while the correct position is illustrated by figure C.

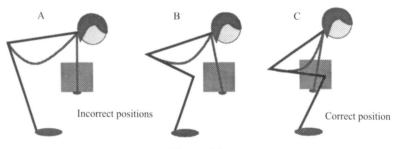

Figure 3.2

Exercises that maintain tone and develop strength in the legs and gluteals will help the pregnant woman cope more easily with bending and lifting tasks during pregnancy; an exercise regime that works these muscles groups should ideally be included two or three times a week with exercises that work abductors, quadriceps, hamstrings, gastrocnemius and gluteals.

Maintaining correct pelvic tilt

The dynamic changes occurring within the pelvic girdle and the increased anterior workload placed on the spinal column results in a forward tilt of the pelvis, causing backache and secondary poor posture. Correcting and trying to maintain a normal pelvic tilt is vital to the well-being and maintenance of good posture in the pregnant woman. The pelvic tilt can be performed standing, kneeling on hands and knees on the floor (in box position) or standing against a wall, especially if the woman has difficulty in grasping the concept of the pelvic tilt.

Technique when standing

* Stand with feet hip distance apart, knees 'soft' (not locked out).

* Place one hand over the abdomen and one hand over the gluteal muscles of the buttocks.
* Now contract the abdominal muscles at the same time as squeezing the gluteal muscles and 'pushing' or tucking the seat underneath, trying to tip the pelvis in towards the body at the front.
* Standing sideways in front of a full length mirror will aid performance of this exercise as a definite 'lift up and in' movement of the uterine contents can easily be seen.
* It is important to breathe out as abdominal and gluteal muscles are contracted. The three T's — tuck, tilt and tighten may help mothers to remember how to perform the exercise and contract muscles, held for 10 seconds before release. It is important to return back to the central starting position and not to throw the seat back as this will increase lordosis, straining the lower back.

Technique when kneeling in the box position

* On hands and knees on a carpeted or covered surface (use towels, blankets or exercise mat if uncovered floor only is available).
* Knees should be directly under hips.
* Hands, flat on the floor, should be underneath shoulders, fingers pointing forwards.
* It is vital that the back should be flat and not allowed to dip or sag throughout the exercise. If it does, this is an indication to stop and rest, as weak muscles, weight of the uterine contents and gravity are creating stresses that the back muscles cannot cope with (see *Figure 3.3*).

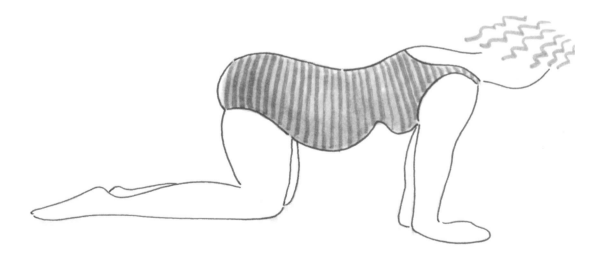

Figure 3.3

* In box position, with a flat back, breathe in.
* On exhalation contract abdominal muscles, push or tuck the bottom underneath. Try to bring the symphysis pubis joint closer towards the baby.

* Hold the contraction if you can for up to 10 seconds.

* As you release try to maintain a flat back position; do not allow the back to hollow.

As the abdominals are working slightly against gravity, more effort is needed for this position, enhancing tone for the rectus abdominis muscle (see *Figure 3.4*).

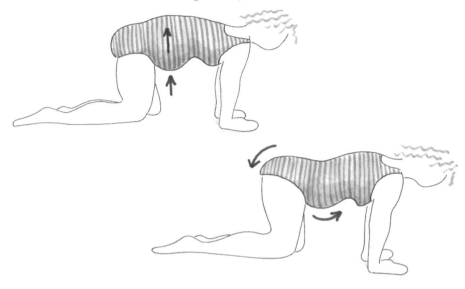

Figure 3.4

Technique when standing against a wall

Standing against a wall usually helps women who have difficulty in grasping the technique of the pelvic tilt.

* Stand as close as possible to a flat wall, back and heels touching the wall.

* Place hands on abdomen in order to feel abdominal tigthening when the rectus is contracted. Because of poor tone or overstretched muscles, especially near to term, some women complain of not feeling any abdominal contraction at all; placing the hands and feeling for the tightening sensation can sometimes aid them.

* Breathe in. On expiration push the small of the back into the wall; try to flatten out the curve in the lower part of the spine.

* At the same time contract the abdominal muscles. Tuck the seat underneath; tilt the pelvis in towards the body.

* Release back to starting position, breathing in ready to perform another pelvic tilt.

4

Structure of a fitness class

An exercise class that is structured to encompass all the desirable elements of physical activity should contain four sections: warm-up; aerobic work; muscular strength and endurance (MSE); and cool-down.

Components of a fitness class	
Warm-up section	Mobility Pulse raiser Short stretch
Aerobic/cardiovascular section	Build up Hard Cool-down
MSE (muscular strength and endurance) section	Muscular strengthening
Cool-down section	Cool-down stretch Relaxation Final mobiliser

Warm-up section

Mobility

Aim: To prepare the body and joints for more strenuous exercise by taking joints through their normal range of movements as the synovial fluid warms up. The warmer it gets, the freer the fluid flows thereby increasing the joint's ability to move with ease. It prepares the cardiovascular system by giving a graduated increase in demand for oxygen. An appropriate warm-up increases blood flow to the muscles. It also allows the participant to rehearse steps or movements that will take place again later in the class. For example, a grapevine step that will be used later in the aerobic section. An effective warm-up helps prevent injury or soreness.

Method: Appropriate mobility movements that incorporate the major joints include:

- shoulder circles
- hip circles
- waist circles
- side bends
- heel/toe touches
- gradual build up of body movements within normal range of joint movement
- half squats.

Effects: The muscle becomes more pliable. It contracts and relaxes faster if warmed up correctly. The haemoglobin releases oxygen more readily if muscles are pre-warmed by exercise. Joints are lubricated in synovial fluid, which enhances the ease and range of movements. Add simple moving steps, eg. walking forwards and backwards, marching on the spot or double side steps in between mobilising the joints.

Pulse raiser

Aim: Part of the 'warming-up' process. A gradual increase in intensity of workload, triggering physiological responses in the body that are needed to cope with the extra demands of the workload.

Method: More dynamic body movements. Use large muscle groups and a greater range of movements. Increase the tempo. Introduce moving steps that may be more complex, eg. grapevine steps, step and touch.

Effect: It increases the pulse, improves oxygen uptake, and increases flow of blood to muscles.

Short stretch

Aim: To ease out the muscle, gently stretching it back to original length.

Method: Short static stretch positions including major muscle groups.

Effect: It eases muscle out to original length. Relaxes muscle after its work and makes it safer to use again.

Aerobic section

Aim: To exercise the cardiovascular system, to improve its efficiency and create a 'training' effect. During pregnancy, maintenance of a fitness level with a gradual easing off of aerobic workload is desirable. Pregnancy is not the time to attempt to improve aerobic fitness levels. The heart grows bigger during pregnancy to cope with the massive cardiovascular changes taking place. The extra two to three stone that many women put on acts as an overload. Therefore, although aerobic work is reduced in intensity and duration fitness levels may be maintained.

Method: Gradually build up intensity and then cool down slowly. Aim for a 15–20 minute work-out in the long term. Use major muscle groups; use dancing, marching, non-impact movements using major muscle groups.

Effects: It strengthens the heart and improves lung capacity and circulation. It helps relieve tension and makes you feel good.

Muscular strength and endurance section

Aim: To improve muscular endurance so that the body can regularly take part in an activity that involves continuous use of muscles.

Method: Usually by using overload principle. FID: frequency, intensity, duration of exercise.

Effect: By exercising the muscles at a higher level than normal they will adapt to the increased workload and operate more efficiently.

During pregnancy, the FID principle of overload is NOT used as pregnancy produces its own natural overload. We aim to maintain, not improve, levels of fitness . For regular exercisers the number of repetitions and positions of the exercises will need to be adapted, for example fewer repetitions and more supported body positions.

Cool-down section

Stretch

Aim: To improve range of movement around a joint, release tension and return muscle to original length.

Method: By use of comfortable, correct stretching techniques within a rhythmic activity or supported position, for example on a chair.

Effects: It releases tension and returns muscles to original length.

Relaxation

Aim: To teach how to relax in order to utilise rest periods antenatally. To help cope during labour. To compensate for the lack of sleep during the postnatal period.

Method: Using pillows and blankets on a suitable floor or chair.

Final mobiliser

Aim: To gently 'waken' the body and mind, in order to prepare for the rest of the day's activities.

Method: Gentle, relaxed, short mobility routine.

Effects: To become mentally alert again prior to leaving class.

Implications of pregnancy on components of a fitness class

Warm-up: because of increased blood volume and vascular bed of the uterus, the pulse rate is elevated. The warm-up needs to be small and gradual.

Lung capacity: in the third trimester this is reduced, therefore the warm-up must be gradual and controlled.

Increase in joints' laxity: the reduction in joint stability may result in overstretching of ligaments therefore mobility and stretching exercises must take the effects of relaxin into consideration.

Centre of gravity changes: this affects balance and body control. Great consideration is needed when planning a change of direction, weight transference and speed of movements.

The following examines each section of an exercise class in greater detail.

Warm-up

This component consists of:

1. A mobiliser that will achieve movement in all the major joints of the body such as the spine, hips, knees, ankles and shoulders.

2. A pulse raiser, more moving, larger body activities that will gradually raise the pulse, preparing the heart and lungs for the work to come in the rest of the class.

3. Short, static stretch, aimed at stretching major muscle groups that have been warmed by activity in order to ease out any tension before continuing any strength, aerobic or stamina exercises.

The aims of the warm-up

1. The desirability of 'warming up' the body prior to exercise is widely acknowledged by applied kineseologists, athletic trainers, health club instructors and other professionals who are responsible for improving, or giving advice on, training and health related fitness principles. The major aim of a warm-up session is to prepare the body adequately to cope with the workload that is to follow, with particular emphasis on the joints, muscles and cardiovascular system.

2. To prepare the body and joints for more strenuous exercise by taking the joints through a normal range of movement, thus spreading synovial fluid within the joint. This encourages bathing of all areas inside the joint capsule, aiding ease and fluidity of movement.

3. To prepare the cardiovascular system (heart and lungs) by gradually increasing the demand for more oxygen. This is a rehearsal for more demanding work. Gradually increasing movement and larger body activity creates an increased blood flow to the muscles. This is a rehearsal of movement that will follow in the cardiovascular section (or aerobic work) part of the class. This will help to prevent injury and stiffness. If muscles are 'warmed up' correctly, they become more pliable, contracting and relaxing more efficiently. Haemoglobin, which carries the oxygen in the blood, releases oxygen more readily if the muscles are pre-warmed by exercise. Muscle fibres contract and relax faster when appropriately prepared for work. A gradual increase in intensity of

workload will trigger physiological responses in the body as a response to the extra demands of the workload. The effect will be an increased pulse rate, an improvement in oxygen uptake and an increase in the flow of blood to the muscles.

The last part of the warm-up involves systematically stretching the warmed muscle groups in order to release tension that may have built up in the warm-up phase. Stretches should be static. There should be no jerk or bounce. Particular care is needed during pregnancy and in the early postpartum period as the effects of relaxin hormone relax ligament and connective tissue, allowing a greater range of movement than normal. During this time it is possible to take a joint beyond its normal range of movement. If ligaments are stretched then the joint is more unstable. Relaxin hormone affects all parts; of the body, its level is highest at 12 weeks gestation and remains so until delivery and for up to three to five months postnatally. Areas at great risk are the pelvis and spine, especially the lumbar region (lower back). Stretches should be held for 8–10 seconds in supported positions that do not dramatically increase workloads on other supporting joints or muscle groups.

The implications of pregnancy on the warm-up

1. During pregnancy there is an elevated pre-exercise heart rate of 10–15 beats per minute above normal resting pulse. This dictates that the warm-up process must be gradual and shorter in length.

2. Remember that relaxin hormone relaxes ligaments and connective tissue, producing potential instability in all joints of the body, especially the pelvis and spinal regions.

3. A pregnant woman's centre of gravity is high, rising, unstable and moves further back in order to maintain balance. This adaptation will affect:
   - balance
   - pace of weight transference
   - pace of change of direction
   - speed of movement
   - control of movement.

4. As maternal core body temperature is raised by 0.5° above normal in pregnancy, the fetus's development may be impaired if hyperthermia is induced by a too vigorous or too prolonged warm-up or a too demanding aerobic section.

5. As pregnancy progresses tiredness and increased girth will dictate workload. Ensure that supported positions are available.

Implications of the warm-up on the joints

Major joints of the body should be mobilised by taking them through a normal range of movement. This encourages:
- less risk of injury during exercise
- enhanced performance of exercise or task by practising the movement first
- the synovial fluid to lubricate the areas of joints and improve ease of movement.

A synovial joint is the place where the meeting of two bones is enclosed in a joint capsule. The ends of the bones are covered with cartilage. The capsule is supported externally by strong fibrous bands called ligaments. Within the capsule is the fluid called synovial fluid. Synovial membrane also lines the inside of the capsule. The ends of the bones, inside the capsule are covered with cartilage, the thickness depending on the stress to which that joint is normally subjected. During warm-up the cartilage absorbs substances from the synovial fluid and swells slightly reducing friction during exercise. This effect is temporary, lasting between 10–30 minutes following exercise. The synovial fluid is encouraged to lubricate all parts of the joint as it is taken through its normal range of movement, facilitating ease of motion.

Major joints of the body to be warmed-up prior to exercise include:

- neck
- shoulders
- spine
- pelvis (hips)
- knees
- ankles.

Effects of the warm-up on the muscles

There are three different types of muscle fibres in the body: cardiac muscle, smooth muscle and skeletal muscle. Skeletal, or striped muscle is surrounded by a layer of connective tissue. Its'purpose is to provide a surface over which other surrounding muscles can slide when contraction and movement takes place. Pre-warmed muscle fibres contract and relax more efficiently and are less prone to injury.

Mobility exercises of the warm-up

Aim: To initiate normal range of movement with major joints of the body in order to promote warm-up effect.

Exercises

Neck

Head turns: 1. Turn the head to alternate sides. Keep the movement smooth.
                            2. Drop ear down towards same side shoulder, then return to central starting position. Keep both shoulders down. Repeat other side.
                            3. Drop ear down towards same side shoulder, slowly sweep chin down on to chest, sweep chin to opposite ear, centralise head.
                                  Repeat each exercise 6–8 times.

Contraindication: to avoid compression of cervical vertebrae do not extend head backwards. Perform with control, do not jerk or perform at speed. Speed reduces control and can result in injury.

Shoulder girdle

Shoulder lifts: Lift shoulder up towards ear, press down away from ear. Alternate each side or lift both shoulders up and push away and down together. Make movement smooth, deliberate and precise.

Shoulder rolls: Pull shoulders forward, lift up towards ear, rotate shoulder back and down to starting position. Alternate sides or do both together.To develop the range of movement place right hand on right shoulder, sweep elbow up and forward, past the head, sweep elbow past the ear, back and down to starting position, increasing range of movement within shoulder joint. Repeat on other side, alternately. Reverse movement by sweeping elbow back in a circular movement to starting position. It is important not to perform these too quickly as speed will probably result in poor technique and loss of control.

Full arm circles: Sweep whole length of arm forward and up, sweep arm past ear and head, back and down, returning to start position. Repeat alternate sides. Finish mobility of shoulder girdle with this full circulation of the shallow shoulder joint that gives a greater range of movement.

Alternative arm swings gradually bringing arms up a little higher. This will slowly increase the range of movement. Include small knee bends with this movement.

'Brush your hair': Take alternate hands and sweep palm from forehead over back and down to nape of neck, taking the elbow back and rotating shoulder joint. Return to the starting position.

You can vary these exercises if you incorporate some of the following:

- slow pace (half time) for shoulder lifts
- quicker pace (full time) for shoulder lifts
- four each side alternating
- lift right then left shoulder. Then depress right and left shoulder
- alternate reaches across the front of the body
- alternate reaches taking the arm up into the air

Spine

Side bends: place the feet hip distance apart, supporting hand on hip. Lift ribcage up away from body and tilt body to same side of supporting hand. Think of it as more of a lift up movement, rather than a lean over. Do not move too far away from midline as the increased effort needed to centralise the longer body axis places stress on fixating muscle groups in torso and pelvic areas. Return to the starting position. Alternate sides when working.

Side twists: place feet hip distance apart, 'soft' knees, tuck seat under and tilt pelvis in towards baby. Lift both arms bending at elbows out of the side of body, lock body into central position. Keep hips facing forwards, as upper body and arms are turned towards one side, and then return to central position. Repeat other side, slow controlled, smooth movements that mobilise the spinal area.You can develop this movement by keeping the feet the same but keeping arms down at sides of body when turning to left and right side. Return to central position.

These exercises can be performed in the seated position. It is best to use a chair as the effort needed to maintain a straight spine while sitting on the floor is considerable for most pregnant women.

Hip and knee joints

Single, alternate side hip hitches: Stand with feet slightly wider than hip distance apart. Keep the knees soft. Tuck seat under, tilt pelvis, tucking baby in towards body. Lift hip bone on right side up towards rib cage on same side. Remember to keep both feet flat on the floor. Return to starting position. Hold for a small pause before repeating on other side, to avoid excessive 'momentum' swing and increased risk of uneven pressure on pelvic girdle. Repeat 6–8 times.

Pelvic circling: Starting position as above. Rotate hip out to one side, circle hips round to back, other side and to the front, ensuring that knee joint is not locked out. When circling to the front, use the power of the abdominal corset muscles to 'pelvic tilt' as you complete a full circular movement. Repeat in the opposite direction in a slow controlled manner. Avoid jerky, fast, uncontrollable momentum that puts pressures on relaxin induced unstable joints within the pelvic girdle. Repeat 3–4 times each side.

Half squats or knee bends: In standing position, take feet a little wider than hip distance apart. Turn the feet so that they are slightly pointing on the diagonal. Bend knees into half squat position, then rise up to starting position, tucking the seat under and tilting baby in towards the body. As you do this make sure that the knee joint stays in line with ankle joint on descent and does not extend beyond, in order to avoid excess pressure on ligaments of the knees. This exercise can be performed standing sideways by an exercise bar, wall or using the back of a chair for support. You may have to stack two or three chairs for taller individuals. This mobilises hip joints, knee joints. Repeat 6–8 times.

Moving half squats: Squat on the spot with single or double side steps in between and back to starting position. Again this mobilises hip joints and knee joints.

Knees lifts: These should be performed only in water based exercise class, not dry site, unless you are using a chair, bar or wall for extra support. The enhanced support of chest deep water ensures stability and reduces risk of poor balance and lack of coordination. Stand with feet slightly turned out, a little wider than hip distance apart. Supporting leg should be 'soft' at the knee joint (slightly bent). Lift knee up and slightly out to the side to compensate for lack of space at front of body. Lift knee as far as is comfortable and take foot back down to floor to starting position. Repeat on other side, 3–4 repetitions on each side.

Pelvis

Pelvic tilts: Standing with the feet hip distance apart keeping the knee joints soft. Remember the three Ts: tuck, tilt, tighten. Tuck the seat or bottom under to prevent lordosis (excessive curvature of the lower spine). Tilt pelvis in towards body, trying to tuck baby in closer. Tighten abdominal muscles while tucking and tilting. Try not to contract gluteal or bottom muscles. Return to standing position, trying not to stick seat out on return to avoid lordosis and further stress on lumbar region of spine. Avoid fast repetitions and stress to the pelvic girdle rendered unstable by relaxin.

Ankle joints

Heel/toe mobiliser: Feet hip distance apart (standing or sitting). Supporting leg should be 'soft' at the knee joint (don't lock the joint out). Perform heel/toe touch movement by alternately lifting foot and placing first heel and then toes of same foot on and into contact with floor surface in front of foot. Try to flex foot with heel contact and point foot with toe contact. Ensure all the movement happens at the ankle joints; isolate the knee joint of the working foot, keeping movements in the knee to a minimum. Repeat 6–8 repetitions each side.

Heel raises: These can be performed either standing or sitting. Place the feet hip distance apart. Make sure that supporting leg is soft at knee joint. Push base of feet down into floor while lifting heels off floor. Return feet to floor. Repeat 6–8 times to help mobilise ankle joint and contract calf muscles (gastrocnemius and soleus). If you are sitting make certain that both feet are comfortably flat on the floor before you begin.

Pulse raising movements of the warm-up

These exercises are intended to raise the pulse gradually, as part of the warm-up process. They can also be used with more intensity and for a longer period of time to work aerobically. Motivation and great fun can be achieved if choreographed to music. Pulse raising movements include the following:

Step touch on the spot

Step touch, moving forwards then backwards to starting position

Double side step to right and left

Double squat side step to right or left. Add biceps curl for variety. A biceps curl is performed by contracting the biceps muscle in the upper forearm. This is achieved by raising the hand and lower arm upwards towards the shoulder joint, flexing the elbow joint and returning the lower arm to the start position

Step touch on the spot with alternate arm reaches forward

March forwards, backwards, on the spot, march into diagonal

March forwards, on the spot, quarter turn then forwards, backwards, quarter turn, repeat

Grapevine step to right or left (step to right, take left foot behind right foot, step to right with right foot and touch left foot on the spot), repeat in opposite direction

Transference of weight on the spot from one foot to the other, bending the knee slightly as weight is transferred from side to side, ensure feet are facing diagonals, slightly wider than hip distance apart

Step touch with alternate hamstring curls (skaters step) on the spot (add a biceps curl as well)

Half squats on the spot, add a biceps curl

Half squats on the spot with arm swings to right or left, sweeping arms to shoulder height

Half squats on the spot with alternate arm swings forwards and backwards, keeping arms to shoulder height

Keep movements simple, low and non-impact and rhythmical. Instil or maintain correct posture throughout the warm-up. Ensure that progressive movements are gradual in build-up.

Stretch during the warm-up

The end of the warm-up section incorporates a stretch component. Remember that relaxin hormone will allow exploitation of increased flexibility around joints. It creates an increased movement range and stretch of supporting ligaments thereby enhancing potential joint instability. Stretches are used to maintain, but not to extend, flexibility; to promote relaxation and remove tension from muscle fibres.

Guidelines for teaching

1. Avoid overstretching.
2. Ensure supported body positions — use chair, side wall, exterior doors, exercise bar.
3. Perform static stretches slowly giving clear instruction on what should be felt and where.
4. Ensure that no breath-holding takes place while stretching.
5. Make sure that muscles have been pre-warmed by pulse raising.

6. Avoid long static periods during stretch where cooling down of muscles occurs.

7. If a cool environment, introduce mobility or pulse raising moves in between stretches if necessary.

Stretches for the upper body

Trapezius (upper back across the shoulders)

Pectoralis major (chest wall) on the front of the body

Sternocleidomastoid (major muscle situated each side of the neck; front view)

Triceps (back of upper arm)

Stretches for the lower body

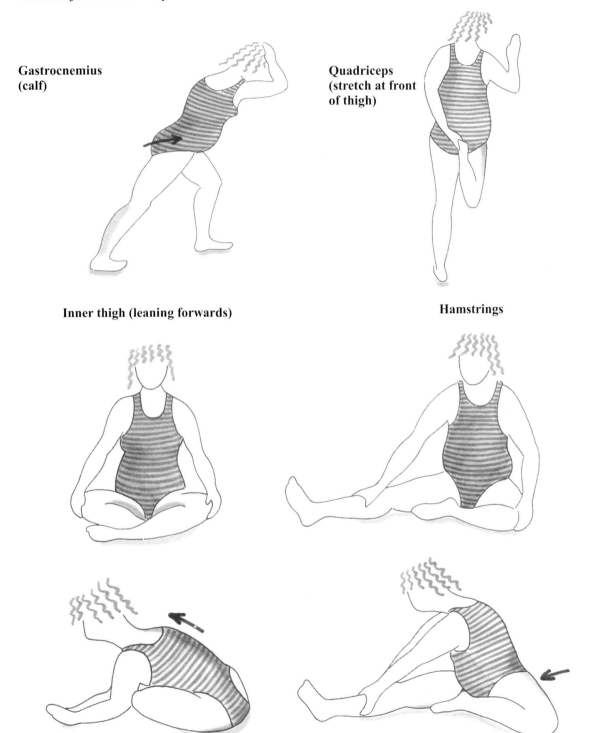

Gastrocnemius (calf)

Quadriceps (stretch at front of thigh)

Inner thigh (leaning forwards)

Hamstrings

Aerobic section

In general the aim of the aerobic or cardiovascular section of a fitness class is to challenge the cardiovascular system in order to produce a training effect by maintaining a pulse rate of 60–65% maximum heart rate. The maximum heart rate is calculated by taking the number 220 and subtracting the individual's age. However, due to pregnancy aerobic pulse rates should not exceed 65% of the maximum heart rate of the individual.

During pregnancy the aim is not to dramatically improve cardiovascular fitness by using the overload principle although previous non-exercisers regularly report that they feel fitter. When training is imposed on the pregnant woman she is able to improve cardiovascular function. Many regular exercisers do not want to lose their fitness levels or gain weight and one of the greatest challenges for the fitness teacher and midwife is to convince the superfit mother who works out four to five times a week that she can and should reduce her workload for the safety of herself and her baby. Even though she is working at a much lower aerobic capacity she can still maintain a fitness level that will be beneficial.

Some research studies (Mittlemark *et al*, 1991) have reported a reduction in blood flow to the uterus and its contents as blood flow is demanded by the major muscle groups, such as the thighs and gluteals, the working muscles demand more oxygen during immediate or advanced physical exercise. This research was carried out on pregnant sheep who were made to work out at 70% MHR: uterine blood flow fell by 21% although it was noted that oxygen supply to the uterus was still maintained at pre-exercise levels. The pregnant woman's body also has many compensatory mechanisms that are triggered by physical, metabolic or hormonal stresses ensuring that oxygen can be transferred to the uterus. Because there is very little research information on the effects of prolonged, demanding aerobic work on the human fetus, instructors during pregnancy must always err on the side of caution. Teachers have the responsibility of two individuals: the mother and the baby. Although professionals now have a window into the uterus by the use of scans, they do not have on-the-spot information of the biophysical profile of the fetus in the uterus. There may be conditions of hypertension or high blood pressure that causes vasoconstriction of the blood vessels in the umbilical cord, thus reducing blood flow to the baby. Inappropriately high levels of aerobic work with the capacity to reduce blood flow even further could again compromise an already at-risk fetus. Nicotine has the same effect on the blood vessels in the cord. Also very anaemic women will have a reduced capacity to carry oxygen in their red cells. The need to screen pregnant women before allowing them to participate in a pregnancy fitness class becomes apparent when such issues are discussed. The condition of a baby can be monitored and often is, by cardiotocography during the antenatal period. This involves monitoring the baby's heart rate and analysing by use of a printout various aspects of heart rate, rhythm and responses to stress stimuli. If a baby is being monitored regularly because of poor CTGs it is a sign that all is not well and aerobic work should be contraindicated. You will find an extract of the American College of Obstetricians Guidelines on exercise in pregnancy in *Chapter 5*, plus some general guidelines that should be taken in to consideration.

Guidelines for aerobic activity

Work for only 15–20 minutes. If the participant is a regular exerciser and fit and the structure and time of the class allows it, design two segments split by 45 minutes.

Vary the intensity of the workload still staying within the parameters of what is appropriate for pregnancy. Work to the beat of the music; use half pace sometimes; incorporate some on-the-spot movements as well as marching on the spot. Vary the pace to give the individual ample opportunity to work at a much lower rate if she needs to, for example during the arm work while marching on-the-spot, make the movements smaller.

Encourage the participants to work at a lower aerobic level by demonstrating it yourself. Remember that pregnant women tire easily especially in the third trimester.

Avoid high impact activities such as jumping, bouncing on-the-spot or jumping jacks. The relaxin effect on the joints can damage them during this type of activity. In fact, this type of high impact activity should be avoided by exercisers as it has little benefit and has a great risk of injury. The pelvic floor also needs to be protected to avoid stress incontinence.

Carefully control speed of movement and directional changes to avoid uncontrollable momentum, poor technique and increased risk of injury. Pregnant women, especially in the third trimester of pregnancy, become more clumsy.

Stay within recommended safety guidelines regarding pulse levels, that is not above 140 beats per minute if aged 20 or over. Reduce to 126 beats per minute if aged 40 or over to avoid potential redistribution of blood flow away from the uterus and the fetus (see *Table 4.1*).

Actively encourage pregnant women to work at their own level during the class; remind them frequently that they should do this by listening to their bodies and how they feel.

If the weather is very hot or humid or the environment is not suitable, for example no windows or air conditioning avoid aerobic work.

Be aware of the possible teratogenetic effects of maternal overheating in the first trimester. When major organs and systems of the fetus are being developed maternal core temperature over 101°F may research states, cause abnormalities in some mammals. At six weeks gestation a crucial period of development of the fetus, some women may not realise that they are pregnant especially if they have irregular periods. Fitness centres should alert women to this danger.

Avoid dehydration by ensuring that maternal pulse rates stay within recommended rates and the length of time worked is between 15–20 minutes. Ensure that plenty of fluids are freely available throughout the class.

If Braxton Hicks contractions occur during or after the aerobic section very carefully monitor or stop the aerobic section. This is especially important for women who have a history of premature labour. Braxton Hicks are usually painless tightening of the uterus. They occur at regular intervals throughout most normal pregnancies and are thought to be a normal physiological process that increases the blood flow to the uterus. Painful prolonged Braxton Hicks during or after the aerobic section could indicate a threat of early labour.

Exercise performance, especially in the first trimester may be affected by nausea, gastrointestinal upsets, lethargy and tiredness. Women should be advised to avoid exercise until these early symptoms have settled.

Hypoglycaemia, or low blood sugar levels is more common in the third trimester. Energy is needed in the form of calories and women should be encouraged to have a light carbohydrate snack two hours before exercising. Not eating could result in faintness and dizziness when exercising.

Avoid prolonged overhead arm movements. These could result in a rise in blood pressure which is not desirable. Keep repetitions down to between six and eight.

The components of the aerobic section are aimed at creating an aerobic curve whereby the pulse is gradually raised to its maximum range for that individual or class and then gradually reduced by the end of the aerobic section. This is acheived by being aware of the use of large muscle groups, predominantly in the lower body. This will demand oxygen from the heart producing a rise in the heart rate.

In pregnancy keep the movements and the choreography simple. This allows the teacher time to teach more effectively and observe more so they are able to adapt the exercise, rate and pace if needed. Promotion of good technique, posture and movement enhances the class. Movements include:

Pulse raising movements

Brisk walking on the spot.

Alternate marching and walking on the spot.

Walking or marching forwards and backwards.

Marching or walking in a diagonal line. To add interest include claps, toe touches to floor etc.

Half squats on the spot: Feet slightly wider than hip distance and pointing diagonally, bend knees into a half squat. Ensure that the knees stay in line with the ankles in order to maintain stability and reduce stress on the joints. Return to the starting position but remember not to lock the knees. These can be performed as double side squats or more stepping to the right or left for two to four beats before returning to the starting position. The deeper the squat the greater the demand on the heart to oxygenate the quadriceps muscle groups in the thighs as they contract as the legs are straightened.

Transfer weight from side to side on the spot. Make sure that the feet are slightly wider than hip distance apart with feet pointing on the diagonal. Bend knees slightly. Transfer the weight of the body over to the right foot. As you do this lift the left foot so that only the tip of the toes touch the floor. Then transfer the weight over to the left side, straighten the knees keeping the right toe in contact with the floor. Repeat on alternate sides. For interest add bicep curls. Or you can reach forwards or upwards with the arms. As you develop add a hamstring curl but not while reaching as this demands agility and balance.

Step touch forward: Walk forward one step leading with the right leg. Bring left leg forward and touch the floor with the toes. Then repeat leading with the left leg. Take 4 of these steps forward and then 4 backwards to return to the starting position.

Swim step: this is useful in an aquanatal class. Take one step forward at a time. As the right foot steps forward use the arms in a breaststroke movement. Pull the arms back as the left leg is brought forward.

Crossed-arms step back: This is a useful movement to return to the starting position after the swim step. Take one step backward at a time. Make sure that the arms are under the water straight out in front of the body with the fingers together. Use the hands as paddles and pull the arms across the front of the body using the resistance of the water to enhance the exercise. This exercise focuses on the pectoral muscle groups.

The pulse raising movements can be used to increase aerobic activity by making the body movements bigger, more pronounced and intense. Deeper squats, the addition of upper arm work and more dynamic reaches forward will contribute to raising the pulse rate to the desired level. Remember that excessive repetitions of the upper body work will raise the blood pressure and result in the type of complications previously discussed. During the aerobic section some of the points to remember include:

- because of fast weight gain and a lower centre of gravity, movements may become clumsy, especially in the third trimester
- resting pulse rate may be 15 beats per minute higher than normal as the heart is already working harder
- because of increased volume of blood, stroke volume increases; hypertrophy of cardiac muscle occurs to compensate
- pelvic floor stress is inevitable due to the weight of the fetus. Changes in direction during a class have more significance due to the increased momentum. Movement must be low impact or non-impact
- If the exercise level is intense lactic acid is produced and this will affect the acidity of the blood. This obviously can harm the fetus. Work out at 60–65% of maximum heart rate for between 15–20 minutes. To calculate your maximum heart rate see *Table 4.1*. Take 220, subtract your age to give you your MHR. Work at 60–65% of this, eg. aged between 20–30 between 110–130 pulse over a minute.

Table 4.1: Maximum heart rates during aerobic component			
Age	**60%**	**65%**	**70%**
20	120	130	140
25	117	126	136
30	114	123	133
35	111	120	129
40	108	117	126
45	105	113	122
Maximum pulse levels taken over a 1 minute count to ensure a safe aerobic workout			

Muscular strength and endurance

Generally, the aim of this section of a fitness class is to improve muscular tone and endurance so that the body can take part regularly in an activity that involves continuous use of muscles, such as gardening or carrying babies, toddlers, shopping and buggies on and off buses. Improving muscle tone during pregnancy can help the pregnant woman to cope with the massive physiological changes taking place. These can include an extra two or three stones of weight and dramatic demands on the spine and posture, and the need to either carry on working, care for other members of the family, or both.

Exercising the body at a level above its normal level results in the system adapting to the increased workload which in turn means that the system operates more efficiently. This is achieved by increasing the frequency, intensity and duration of the exercises. This is sometimes known as the 'overload principle'. This principle is not utilised during pregnancy, although there will be improvement seen for many women who have never exercised before. However, pregnancy is not the time to embark on a rigorous, demanding exercise regime. The aim is to maintain or develop strength and endurance in major muscle groups, to promote correct posture, to develop body awareness and control and to maintain muscle tone, thereby improving body image.

Pregnancy implications for MSE section

1. The destabilising effect of relaxin hormone on joints will affect exercise technique. It will also dictate how and in what position exercises should be taught.

2. Isometric or static contraction of muscles (where the body parts do not move, and there is no shortening of muscle fibre during the contraction phase) create a rise in blood pressure. Minimise this type of exercise as much as possible. Some isometric contraction occurs when fixator muscles statically contract while the prime move contracts, eg. deltoid muscles on the shoulders statically contract while holding up the arms in order to perform pec deck exercises (pectorals major muscles being the prime mover).

3. Supine hypotensive syndrome will affect what position the pregnant woman can safely work in. A drop in blood pressure that can cause a reduced blood flow to the uterus and baby will be the result when a pregnant woman lies flat on her back. This occurs because the pregnant uterus falls back into major blood vessels returning blood to the heart, thereby reducing the blood flow to the uterus. Because of this, women should not lie flat on their backs after 16 weeks gestation. This has implications for abdominal work, making abdominal curl exercises an unsuitable exercise after 16 weeks gestation.

4. As pregnant women tire easily, especially in the third trimester, or much sooner if discomfort contributes to poor sleeping patterns, consideration needs to be given to positions of support, and alternatives, when exercising the various muscle groups throughout the body.

5. Work from a well supported base at all times. Provide the back of a chair, stacked to an appropriate height if necessary for the taller woman, exercise bars, walls, chairs to sit on, or an appropriate floor (carpeted or exercise mats). Do not use a 'partner' to provide support for pregnant women, expecially if they are both working out at the same time. They cannot concentrate on their technique if they are also trying to support a heavily pregnant body. Chairs are both very useful and easily available. Exercise routines can be performed very successfully using the chair as the base, not only for support, but also for the choreography if music is being used. Start by standing behind the chair, performing squats, move to the side to work, for example, the gluteals in side leg raises, then sit on the chair and finish with straight leg extensions to work the quadriceps muscles at the front of the thigh.

Sitting on the floor can be very demanding on the muscles in the spine and lower back. Beware of using this support for prolonged periods. If pec decks are performed in a cross-legged sitting position on the floor, give frequent rests in between six or eight repetitions. By allowing the back to 'slump' a little and by using the hands as support to allow the pregnant women to lean back, the back muscles are allowed to relax and tension is removed. This is definately a position that, if prolonged, will be uncomfortable for most pregnant women, so use it for short periods only, with plenty of rest 'positions' in between.

Avoid uneven pressure on the pelvic girdle, hip bones and lower spine. This area of the body is at great risk, not only because of the effect of relaxin hormone, but because of the increased pressure on joints caused by the growing baby. This causes a reduction in the support provided by the abdominal corset to the lumbar region of the spine. Great consideration needs to be given to position for exercising, in order to reduce the stress on these joints as much as possible.

Remember that while performing side leg raises with the right leg, the left leg and hip joint will be taking the whole weight of the body. Static contraction will be occurring in the muscle groups of the left leg, increased pressure will be building in the left hip joint. For these reasons, repetitions of exercises should be between six to eight in number before changing body position and moving on to exercise a different set of muscles. A return to that set of muscles and that exercise can be incorporated into the exercise regime planned by the teacher.

The symphyis pubis joint is affected by relaxin hormone and plays an important role in the stability of the pelvic girdle. It is well known that separation of the SP joint is a common phenomenon but in some women it becomes pathological when this partial separation occurs beyond the usual range. Pain will be a predominant feature on walking or resting. Be aware that the muscles on the inside of the thighs are attached to the symphysis pubis, where the two sides of the pelvic girdle meet at the front of the body. Poor technique, lack of support, and raising the leg too high while performing side leg raises can put more pressure on this joint. Care must be taken to instill, monitor, and reinforce good technique. If pain develops, or is present, advice should be sought from the midwife, physiotherapist or GP. Weight bearing exercise should be discontinued. An aquanatal class would take the effects of gravity away from the pelvic region, and even if exercise was not possible, the support of the water environment, education from the midwife and social support of other pregnant women could still be very useful to such women. Exercising in a water based class is more suitable for pregnant women who have severe backache, once any pathological reasons for backache have been excluded. The support of water and the reduction in pressure on joints make it a much easier environment for them to exercise specific muscle groups. As the abdominal corset plays a key role in supporting the lower back, pelvic tilting and abdominal contractions should be encouraged, in order to try to maintain some tone in the abdominal muscles.

6. It is important to exercise all major muscle groups in order to help the pregnant body adapt and cope with the increasing workload produced by the extra weight and changes in centre of gravity and posture. These include the deltoids in the shoulder region, the chest muscles, and biceps in the upper arm to help with lifting and carrying, something that pregnant and newly delivered women will be doing a lot of. The abdominal corset is of special interest to most

women, pregnant or not, and a whole chapter has been devoted to this region. Bending and lifting techniques during pregnancy and the postnatal period should have the advantage of well-toned muscles that allow correct techniques to be utilised. Exercise the quadriceps, the hamstrings, the gluteals and the calf muscles in the lower body.

7. If weights have been used to enhance exercise performance prior to pregnancy, the weights should be reduced to light hand-held weights only for the experienced, regular exerciser. High resistance exercises, produced by heavy weights, will stress unstable joints and affect blood pressure especially if technique is poor and breath holding is used.

8. Speed, range of movement and exercise technique are very important in maintaining an exercise regime that stops within safe limits for pregnant or postnatal women. For the first three months of pregnancy the regular exerciser can maintain her MSE programme provided that she feels fit and well and has no further obstetric or medical complications. After this time, a gradual reduction in weights, workload and intensity should be encouraged.

When planning which muscle groups are to be exercised and teaching that section of the class remember to:

- avoid performing exercises too fast and without muscle control
- avoid too many repetitions of any exercise
- avoid jerking or bouncing movements
- avoid forcing any movement
- avoid over-exertion, listen to your body, rest whenever you need
- provide supported body positions.

Component considerations

1. Directional changes in terms of the pace and mode.
2. Beware of abdominal twisting.
3. No isometric contraction.
4. Use only four to eight repetitions per muscle group with rests in between. Leg work repetitions could be increased depending on body position.
5. When raising arms above head blood pressure rises. Keep to four to eight repetitions.
6. Perform any pelvic movements in slow, controlled fashion due to increased mobility of joints. Be aware of sacro-iliac joints and the symphysis pubis joint. Avoid excess stress in these areas.
7. Pay particular attention to posture, how to avoid lordosis how to correct standing position.

Stretch

When a muscle is stretched, the so-called stretch reflex makes it contract not relax. This is why a stretch should be slowly 'eased' into and held for a number of seconds in order that the muscle fibres gradually relax and allow the 'stretch' to occur. Some general considerations follow on from the implications that pregnancy has on the 'stretch' part of a fitness class. The reasons why we need to work on flexibility are:

- to improve posture
- to improve our performance of everyday tasks and sports
- to help prevent injury.

Flexibility is limited by:

- the shape of the joints
- ligaments and tendons
- muscles.

The aim of the stretch is to increase the present range of movement. We do this through:

- stretches to lengthen the muscle
- slow, static stretching
- comfortable positions
- stretching to a point of mild tension.

Guidelines for stretching:

1. Stretch only when warm.
2. Stretch only to a point of mild tension not agony.
3. Stretch one muscle group at a time.
4. Stretch in a comfortable position.
5. Always move slowly into a stretch.
6. Hold the stretch statically.

Implications of pregnancy on the stretch section of the class:

1. Relaxin hormone will allow exploitation and enhance flexibility and joint instability.
2. Use stretch to promote relaxation and remove tension from muscle at the end of the warm-up.
3. Use to prevent injury.
4. Use static, held stretches for 6–8 seconds.
5. Use to maintain but not extend mobility and flexibility.
6. Use as part of the cool-down.

Guidelines for teaching

1. Avoid developmental stretch.
2. Provide comfortable body positions for pregnancy.
3. Perform static stretch slowly with clear instruction on what should be felt and where.
4. Ensure that breath is not held.
5. Make sure muscles are warm enough.
6. Avoid long static periods during stretch where cool-down occurs quickly.
7. Introduce mobility if necessary in between stretches.

Strengthen then stretch the following muscles/muscle groups:

- pectorals
- triceps
- hamstring
- adductors/abductors

- trapezius
- gluteals
- quadriceps
- gastrocnemius

Cool-down section

As the warm-up encourages a gentle progressive increase in workload so the cool-down section does the opposite. Stopping abruptly after exercise allows waste products to remain in the bloodstream and muscle (eg. lactic acid) and this can cause discomfort in the body. Gradually decreasing the workload, easing out muscles in slow static stretches followed by a period of rest and relaxation is a necessary and enjoyable part of a pregnancy fitness class or aquanatal class.

Following the muscular strength and endurance section of the class, the muscle groups exercised will need to be gently stretched in order to remove tension from the muscles and promote relaxation. Suitable music can make this part of the class most enjoyable, especially if a few minutes relaxing in a prone or seated position follow on directly.

Relaxin hormone will allow a greater range of movement to occur around joints, so great care should be taken not to overstretch. Flexibility is also limited by the shape of the joints, ligaments and tendons and muscles. If exercisers were not pregnant, developmental stretches (taking the stretch position beyond the normal range of movement) would be encouraged in order to promote greater flexibility and reduce the risk of injury. This is not desirable during pregnancy or the early postnatal period as potential destabilisation of joints can occur.

Implications of pregnancy on stretching in the cool-down section

1. Relaxin hormone is present, affecting joint stability by relaxing the connective tissue and ligaments that attach muscle to bone.
2. As pregnancy progresses, positions in which to stretch will be dictated to a degree by girth discomfort and the amount of fat deposited in various parts of the body as well as the muscle that needs to be stretched out.
3. Pregnant women are more clumsy, cannot see their feet and do not balance as well. This has implications for positions that can be safely adopted when stretching.
4. Successive or multiple pregnancies have higher relaxin hormone levels, thus putting multiparous women more at risk of overstretching.
5. Remember that bouncing or jerky movements when stretching will inhibit the stretch reflex and the muscle fibres will not relax.
6. Muscles must be 'warmed up' before they are stretched, do not stretch 'cold'.
7. Stretches are used to maintain but not to extend mobility and flexibility during pregnancy.
8. Stretches should be moved into slowly and held for six to eight seconds. Ensure that no 'breath holding' occurs, normal respiration should take place throughout.

9. As the stretch is performed, clear instruction should be given on what should be felt and where.

10. Provide comfortable, supported body positions while stretching.

11. Try to avoid long static periods during the stretch component where the body cools down quickly. If necessary, introduce some mobility movements in between stretches.

Relaxation technique

After stretching out the relevant muscle groups relaxation techniques can be taught in a variety of ways. Supine hypotensive syndrome will dictate that a back lying position in which to relax is not appropriate. Preparing to relax is always easiest after some form of exercise, when muscles are slightly fatigued. If at home, try to ensure privacy, take the telephone off the hook, wear loose, comfortable clothing, remove shoes. The ability to relax deeply is an important skill. It is free, always available and gives a feeling of total well-being. There are many ways of achieving relaxation using breathing techniques or visualisation. I have included a relaxation technique that has been successfully used many times. Adopt it as a guide, plagiarise it, or use it to develop other methods. Positions in which to relax include:

* **The recovery position**: lie on your side on the floor. Bring the top knee forward so that it is touching the floor in front. Slightly bend the lower leg lying on the floor. Tuck the bottom arm behind, top arm in front on the floor. Use pillows under the head and breasts, also under the top knee that is in front. Wriggle around until comfortable.

* **Sitting**: sit in a chair, ideally with arms. Ensure that both feet are flat on the floor. If not, provide a lumbar support that will push the seat of the bottom further forward, allowing the feet to rest flat on the floor or provide a stool for feet.
Alternatively, sit on a chair and lean forward onto a support, eg. table or worktop. Rest head on forearms. Put supportive pillows across the knee to give more support and comfort when leaning forward.
Or, sit on the floor, leaning against a wall, pillows behind the lower back, legs can be straight out in front with feet relaxed, turning out slightly OR bend the knees up, with feet flat; whichever is preferred.

* **Floating in the swimming pool**: use floats to push down the back of swimsuits to give extra support. Also, use hand held polystyrene floats under each arm to aid floating. In the pool environment floating on one's back is not a problem as gravity and the weight of the pregnant uterus does not occlude the blood flow to the uterus. Large rubber tyres, which many pools now have, are wonderful to relax in. Blow-up neck floats are a superb aid to the relaxation process. The environment is important. Ensure that the temperature is suitable. A cold swimming pool or a very humid, hot room are obviously not conducive to feeling comfortable.

Now that you have chosen your position to relax in, let's start by taking a few deep breaths in and out. As you inhale deeply, try not to tense any part of your body. Breathe in slowly through your nose. As you breathe out, try to make your breath out longer than your breath in. Do not tense your body by forcing the air out, let the breath just slowly seep out of your nose. As you take that deep breath in, concentrate your mind on what it feels like inside your body. Take pleasure in experiencing, maybe for the first time, the sensation of your lungs expanding fully, of your rib cage lifting up and out. As you breathe out, I want you to imagine that you are breathing out tension and stress that has built up within you and around your baby. Try to visualise this stress leaving your body, use your breath out as a cleansing breath. Remember, make your breath out longer than your breath in each time, allowing that cleansing breath to work for you and your baby.

As you start to relax, you will notice that your breathing will become much less deep, more shallow, a sure sign that your body is starting to relax. Remember, make that breath out longer each time. As tension recedes from your body, resistance between your supporting surface and you becomes less you may feel as though you are moulding into the floor, chair or bed. Allow yourself to float in that warm embrace of relaxation. As you become more and more deeply relaxed, you may notice something else happening. After that long breath out, you may experience a little gap before you need to breathe in again. Allow the music to wash around you, within you, over you.

It is important to wake the body up slowly and gently. Gently tighten the muscles in your legs, from the top of your thigh right down to your ankles, then release them. Tighten the muscles around your bottom muscles around your baby, squeeze and release them. Take in a few more deep breaths and open your eyes.

If you are lying on your side, use your hands to push yourself slowly into a sitting position. If you are sitting in a chair, slowly lift your head back to a central position. If you are relaxing in your bath, bend one knee at a time and place your feet flat on the bottom of your bath and using your handrails pull yourself into a sitting position. A safe way of getting up from the floor when you are pregnant is to turn on to the hands and knees, bring one knee forward with your foot flat on the floor. Now, use that thigh as a lever to push yourself up from the floor into a standing position.

Posture check prior to mobilisation

Stand with your feet hip distance apart, knees slightly soft, not locked out. Tuck your bottom underneath and tilt your pelvis forwards, getting rid of that hollow in your lower back. Lift your ribcage up, ease your shoulders back to a central position, arms hanging loosely by your side. We are now going to mobilise all the major joints in your body, to revitalise, loosen up and prepare for the day's activities.

5

Screening and safety aspects

This chapter focuses upon the importance of screening participants for and the aspects of safety of exercise. Later in the chapter the section 'Guidelines for teaching' illustrates a list of considerations that an exercise instructor will need to incorporate into her class and environment, in order that the structure, content and environment is safe for the pregnant and postnatal exerciser. The necessity for screening each participant before allowing them to join a class is vital. The American College of Obstetricians and Gynaecologists has produced a list of contraindications to exercise in pregnancy.

The American College of Obstetricians guidelines to exercise during pregnancy

If appropriate guidelines are followed, it is safe to assume that healthy pregnant women can maintain levels of aerobic fitness and muscular strength and endurance without any detriment to the fetus or mother. Appropriate, regular, ongoing screening before participation and during the duration of exercise classes by a qualified teacher with a specialised knowledge base of exercise during pregnancy should ensure that any risks are kept to a minimum for the vast majority of pregnant exercisers. Although the physiological changes that take place in the body during pregnancy and their impact on an exercise regime have been discussed in some detail, it is useful to summarise contraindications. These are:

Absolute contraindications:
- active myocardial disease
- congestive heart failure
- rheumatic heart disease (class ii and above)
- thrombophlebitis
- recent pulmonary embolism
- acute infectious disease
- at risk for premature labour, incompetent cervix, multiple gestations
- uterine bleeding, (or broken waters)
- intrauterine growth retardation or macrosomia
- severe isoimmunisation
- severe hypertensive disease

- no prenatal care
- suspected fetal distress.

Relative contraindications (patients may be engaged in medically supervised programmes):

- essential hypertension
- anaemia
- thyroid disease
- diabetes mellitus
- breech presentations in the last trimester
- excessive obesity or extreme underweight
- history of sedentary lifestyle.

Additional contraindications should be left for the physician to evaluate.

Many pregnant women will be naturally screened out by the very nature of the medical disorder and most will probably be under the expert clinical care of consultant, physician and midwife.There are further questions to be considered when devising a screening questionnaire. The information required other than personal details includes the following:

- number of weeks pregnant
- what gravida (how many times pregnant)
- any problems with this pregnancy
- any problems with past pregnancies
- any medical illness (eg. diabetes, epilepsy)
- taking any medicines or tablets
- joint, muscle, bone injuries
- treatment for any joint, muscle or bone injuries
- surgery within the last 12 months.

If the answer to any of the questions is yes, then a more detailed interview will highlight whether or not the individual:

- is able to exercise
- is able to exercise with specific modifications (eg. anaemic, so no aerobic work at present)
- needs further specialist medical advice (eg. diabetic, twin pregnancy)
- should not exercise at the moment (eg. recent in vitro fertilisation and pregnancy not established, severe pain over symphysis pubis joint on walking).

It is necessary to ascertain regularly, within a group of exercising pregnant women, what their health and obstetric status is. This can be done by encouraging them to keep the exercise teacher up-to-date with progress of their pregnancies and with any developments that may affect their ability to exercise.

General contraindications to exercise during pregnancy:

- pain of any kind
- uterine contractions

- vaginal bleeding/leaking liquid
- dizziness, faintness
- shortness of breath
- palpitations, tachycardia
- persistent nausea and vomiting
- back pain
- pubic or hip pain
- difficulty in walking
- oedema
- decreased fetal activity
- poor cardiotocography (CTG) read out
- reduced fetal growth (IUGR).

Mittlemark, Wisewell and Drinkwater (1991) illustrate the relative contraindications as follows:

- hypertension
- anaemia or other blood disorders
- thyroid disease
- diabetes
- cardiac arrhythmia or palpitations
- history of precipitous labour
- history of intrauterine growth retardation
- history of bleeding during present pregnancy
- breech presentation in the last trimester
- excessive obesity
- extreme underweight
- history of three or more spontaneous abortions
- ruptured membranes
- premature labour
- diagnosed multiple gestation
- incompetent cervix
- bleeding or a diagnosis of placenta previa
- diagnosed cardiac disease.

They also illustrate absolute contraindications as follows:

- pain
- bleeding
- dizziness
- shortness of breath
- palpitations
- faintness
- tachycardia

- back pain
- pubic pain
- difficulty in walking.

Factors to consider when devising exercises for a pregnant woman:

- screening procedure
- sensible footwear and clothing (supportive and loose)
- provide fluids throughout whole session
- warm-up and cool-down periods vital
- when working aerobically ensure that maternal pulse rates do not exceed 60—65% of the maximum heart rate (see chart on *page 37*)
- pulse check during aerobic component
- ensure that the room is well ventilated
- give alternative exercises throughout
- actively encourage working at own level.

Guidelines for teaching

Some considerations for teachers

- know your routine well — you may need to adapt and change it
- quality of voice, focus upon the volume
- music volume — is it for motivation or to create an atmosphere?
- cueing to indicate changes to the participants — use words, body actions, own body movement quality
- starting position — is it time to change position?
- room hazards, eg. chairs, bags, shoes, open windows, shoe laces undone
- organising the group and moving them
- floor, is it carpet, tiling, wood?
- chairs — are they available for use as supports?
- ventilation
- heating
- suitable footwear and clothing
- position of teacher — can you be seen at all times by participants?
- availability of toilets.

Focus of screening

The focus of the screening procedure should be threefold, ie. to check for:

- maternal risks
- fetal risks
- infant risks.

Maternal risks

- injuries to joints and bones
- stress on the cardiovascular system
- premature labour
- hypoglycaemia
- spontaneous abortion
- dehydration.

Injuries to joints and bones

There is a potential injury threat if classes are not low impact in structure, appropriately paced and do not account for relaxin affected joints and alternative supportive body positions are not offered during the exercise sessions.

Stress on the cardiovascular system (heart and lungs)

Reduce running and jogging programmes to two miles a day or less and do not embark on these type of activities as a beginner once pregnant. Ensure appropriate supportive footwear is worn and choose a route that is flat terrain, reducing risk of twisting ankles or stumbling. Reduce risk of redistribution of blood flow by ensuring that target heart rates are at safe levels (no more than 140bpm).

Premature labour

When being physically active, levels of certain substances in the body will rise significantly, namely epinephrine and norepinephrine. Epinephrine inhibits uterine muscle activity and norepinephrine increases the frequency and strength of contractions. If a woman has a history of premature labour or experiences painful Braxton Hicks after the aerobic component, she should be advised to omit aerobic work from her regime and be carefully monitored throughout the rest of the class.

Hypoglycaemia

Generally, during pregnancy glucose levels and fasting blood glucose levels are lower than in the woman who is not pregnant. Carbohydrates are burned up as a source of fuel more quickly during exercise when pregnant. Avoid prolonged intense periods of exercise and ensure a high carbohydrate snack, for example sandwiches and a glass of milk, is taken one to two hours before exercising. Do not exercise on an empty stomach, especially early in the day if nausea and vomiting have prevented breakfast from being eaten.

Spontaneous abortion

Long, intense periods of exercise can cause dehydration, increased production of catecholamine, stress and potential abortion. However, there is no data to prove that any level of exercise can cause spontaneous abortion. Many pregnant women, in the past, have become engaged in very vigorous exercise programmes without aborting. Catecholamines are broken down by the placenta or after birth very efficiently because of high levels of enzymes and usually only 10–15% of catecholamines ever reach the fetus. Catecholamines can affect fetal circulation by reducing maternal blood flow to the uterus. Commonsense advice to avoid these potential threats is to follow carefully the guidelines for aerobic work during pregnancy therefore work for approximately 15 minutes with a pulse rate no higher than 140 beats per minute, and ensure that the temperature of the exercise is not prohibitive by providing adequate ventilation and fluids to drink throughout. In very warm, hot or humid weather do not participate in aerobic work.

Dehydration

Dehydration should occur only if guidelines to length and integrity of the workload are not followed or the exercise environment is not adequately ventilated. Heart rate and therefore core maternal temperature are directly related to the intensity of the exercise. Maternal core temperature should not rise above 38.5°C as 39°C or more in the first trimester may put the fetus at risk of teratogenesis (abnormal development). Do not exercise if symptoms of headache, poor coordination or nausea occur. Stop and rehydrate immediately, especially if the weather is very warm.

Fetal risks

- fetal distress
- intrauterine growth retardation (IUGR)
- prematurity
- fetal malformations.

Fetal distress

Fetal heart rates almost always rise after exercise during pregnancy, although occasionally they may decrease.Ensure that exercise sessions and aerobic work are not intense. Most fetal heart rates are back to their pre-exercise level 15–30 minutes after the exercise period has finished. If there is a history of poor or low fetal movements, or cardiotocography tracings are being regularly monitored to assess the well-being of baby, do not engage in aerobic work or intense periods of strength training that could potentially divert blood away from the uterus to the working muscles.

Intrauterine growth retardation (IUGR)

Women who exercise at high levels throughout pregnancy gain less weight, have lighter babies and tend to deliver earlier by an average of about eight days.Although many factors can contribute to low birth weight babies, intense exercise during pregnancy can have a detrimental effect upon the baby. Research shows that animals who are worked extensively under laboratory conditions also produce lighter newborn. Careful monitoring of the workload, ongoing assessment throughout pregnancy and adaptation to each pregnant woman's particular needs will reduce the risk of inappropriate levels of work, and potential IUGR.

Prematurity

The risks of a premature baby will depend on how pre-term the infant is. Frequently there will be increased risks of breathing disorders (respiratory distress syndrome) jaundice, low birth weight and hypothermia to name but a few.Women who have experienced premature births in the past or who experience painful Braxton Hicks (abdominal tightenings) after any exercise session should cease their exercise activity and be carefully monitored throughout any other exercise activity.

Fetal malformations

High maternal core body temperature of 39°C or higher during the developmental stages of pregnancy are thought to be associated with neural tube defects in the fetus (such as spina bifida or anencephaly).

The problem is that many regular exercisers who work at high intensity would not be aware that they were pregnant in those first few vital weeks of development, particularly if their periods were irregular. Fitness centres and instructors should be aware of this potential threat in early pregnancy and take steps to ascertain that exercisers who think they might be pregnant or who intend to conceive take specific advice as soon as they are able in relating to the intensity and length of their workload.

Infant risks

- less body fat at birth
- increased risk of hypothermia (low body temperature).

These have been discussed under the heading prematurity and IUGR.

Guidelines for screening

Miscarriage

Ask how many the woman has had. If one miscarriage occurred in the first trimester (a common occurrence) then wait until this pregnancy is well established (20–22 weeks). If no problems have occurred, then embark on a pregnancy fitness class or aquanatal class. If two or more miscarriages have occurred, wait until 32+ weeks providing that the pregnancy has been uneventful. In the meantime, aquanatal classes can provide a less demanding regime in the water and may be more appropriate for a woman with this history. If she does not want to exercise or has an antenatal history of problems, she can still kick a float around in the pool and enjoy the social aspects of the class, even if not participating.

Breech presentation

As a large number of pregnancies are breech presentation at 28 weeks gestation it would seem to suggest that, if the ACOG guidelines are followed, a large number of women may not be able to exercise; this may be because a breech presentation may present uneven pressure in the uterus, especially during the last trimester. When the fetus increases its weight threefold, spontaneous rupture of membranes is more likely with the ensuing problems of prematurity. To date I have not found any research data that backs up the statement that breech presentations are a contraindication to exercising. The water environment of an aquanatal class removes the risk of impact and for ten years I have exercised pregnant women with breech presentations in swimming pools with no apparent detrimental effects.

Nausea and vomiting

Refrain from exercising until this has settled. A reduced calorie intake is probably also present and exercising needs an appropriate level of energy to avoid hypoglycaemia and dehydration.

Anaemia

Regular screening tests throughout pregnancy and in the postnatal period should detect low haemoglobin levels (10g or less). Iron therapy can be commenced after consultation with the midwife and general practitioner. Anaemia will have a great effect on a pregnant woman's ability to exercise, especially aerobically, so regular reminders to inform the exercise teacher if anaemia does develop are important.

Carpal tunnel syndrome

Tingling and numbness in the fingers and hands can occur quite early on in pregnancy and can be as little as a tingling sensation in the morning or as much as three or more fingers numb and no ability to grip. Although mechanically the carpal tunnel is in the wrist region, the problem can be triggered by poor posture and originate in the shoulder region. Advice on correct posture can help alleviate some symptoms. In some cases extra support or hand braces are required and referral to the physiotherapy department will result in expert advice and treatment. Any exercise necessitating support in the hands and knees position (or box position) will need to be modified (eg. press ups or static abdominal contraction) by altering the exercise position or standing and using a wall, thus taking pressure off the wrist joints.

Participation in fertilisation programmes

Women who have had great difficulty in conceiving need special monitoring and advice. Generally, I would advise that they do not participate at all until the pregnancy is very well established. Although we know that if guidelines are adhered to exercise does not cause miscarriage, these women may suffer enormous guilt if after a third and finally successful attempt at in vitro fertilisation they then go on to abort having taken part in an exercise regime. They should consult with their consultant, GP and midwife and after 30 weeks of an uneventful pregnancy, be welcomed into your class with full screening and ongoing observation throughout the rest of the pregnancy.

Multiple pregnancies

Hormone levels, especially relaxin, may be raised even further and their ensuing effect on ligaments and joint stability further exacerbated by the increased weight, girth and uterine (or womb) contents of two or more babies. Ideally, women should be given advice and participate in exercise classes as soon as they are pregnant in order to establish appropriate guidelines concerning bending, lifting, back care and exercise technique. The sooner this information is instilled the better. Women with multiple pregnancies stand a great risk of anaemia, breathlessness, tiredness and potential risk of injury during exercise. A carefully screened and monitored pregnant exerciser who starts class participation in the first trimester may be able to participate until 28–30 weeks despite the need for adaptation or reduction in workload in her pregnancy fitness class, but this will be a very individual decision. More support for strength work should be given, for instance sitting on a chair, rather than standing, and omitting aerobic work as soon as she can no longer hold a conversation while working aerobically without becoming breathless. It is probably wise not to allow a woman with a multiple pregnancy who has not exercised into a pregnancy fitness class if she is beyond 24 weeks gestation. After 28–30 weeks, some women will need to omit the aerobic section of the class and just continue with strength work by exercising muscle groups that will help them to adjust to the extra weight and stress placed on the body, especially the spine. Stretch should be limited to short held static stretches that do not exploit the effects of relaxin hormone and exacerbate the threat of destabilising joints. Water based fitness classes can provide extra support and would benefit women with multiple pregnancy as the water environment reduces the effect of gravity, the exercise is not weight bearing and the spine is released of much of its workload, especially if in chest-deep water, an ideal medium for pregnant women to exercise in. When planning pregnancy fitness classes you will need to consider the following:

✱ *Hypertension (high blood pressure)*: It is interesting to note that in individuals who are not pregnant, prescriptive exercise may be advocated as an aid to reducing high blood pressure. One of the physiological responses of the body to a gradual 'warm-up' session is that the arteries and blood vessels dilate in order to pump more blood to the muscles demanding it, thus reducing the blood pressure within. One of the physiological responses of immersion in chest-deep water is for blood pressure to be reduced. I have exercised pregnant women who have had hypertension only (no proteinuria or oedema) in aquanatal sessions, with the permission and knowledge of their general practitioners and have screened their blood pressure recording before, during and after immersion. In all women (about 20 in total) their diastolic recording dropped between 5–10 mm of mercury. Although it is impossible and inappropriate to use these findings in any other way other than anecdotally, it would be interesting for a piece of research to be carried out looking at the efficacy of exercise and immersion in water as a first line treatment. As the renal filtration rate is also increased when immersed in water, physiological and pathological oedema associated with hypertensive disease of pregnancy may be improved. Generally, hypertensive women need to discuss the issue of exercising with their consultant obstetrician, general practitioner or midwife and exercise teacher in some detail. Each individual case will be different and if other problems such as IUGR, poor CTG tracing and poor fetal movements are also present, it would be prudent to exclude women with such histories from exercise classes as the blood supply to the uterus may already be impaired and the extra demands made on the body by exercising may place further strain on the contents (ie. afterbirth and baby) of the uterus; such women can still be given valuable advice on lifting, carrying and walking in order to exercise, and postnatal advice.Individual consultation with the pregnant woman and her medical and midwifery team is vital if hypertension during pregnancy develops. Medical advice must be sought and documented.

✱ *The environment:*

♦ is there adequate ventilation, windows, air conditioning or fans. Is there some form of heating available for colder weather?

♦ be careful about exercising with tights or socks on even if the flooring, carpeting, tiles or wood block are fine as it could be slippery and dangerous. Ensure that the floors have not been polished. If windows open sideways, be aware of the limitation of space and potential threat of impact while working

♦ ensure that the toilets are nearby and a telephone for emergency use or to call for aid if necessary. Have local hospital numbers readily available

♦ provide fluids freely throughout the class especially in warm or hot weather

♦ ensure supports are available, for example chairs, exercise rail, pillows and blankets.

* *Clothing:*

- needs to be loose and non-restrictive. Footwear should be flat and supportive. There are advantages to wearing no footwear if the floor surface is appropriate and a non-impact structure has been adhered to, as a greater range of movement may be achieved, especially if the environment is warm or physiological oedema (swelling) is present in the ankles.
- a well supporting bra needs to be worn at all times throughout pregnancy.

6

Kinesiology — how muscles work and contract

Kinesiology

The three types of muscle tissue are:
- cardiac muscle
- involuntary muscle — not under control of will
- voluntary or skeletal muscle.

A single voluntary muscle consist of bundles of muscle fibres, giving bulk and shape, enveloped in a sheath of fibrous tissue. For movement to occur, origin and insertion of the muscle must move closer together. Muscles will atrophy if not used. Muscles need to cross a joint for movement to occur. Points to note about muscles include the following:
- many muscle fibres lie parallel to each other and in bundles
- some are thicker than others
- they vary in length
- muscles contain varying numbers of muscle fibre
- once stimulated all muscle fibres will contract
- when lifting a weight the appropriate number of muscle fibres required will contract and those fibres not used will remain inactive
- at rest, there is always slight contraction called 'tone'.

Muscular strength component

Aims

1. To maintain or develop strength or endurance in major muscle groups.
2. To promote good posture.
3. To develop body awareness and control.
4. To maintain and develop muscle tone, improving body image.

Pregnancy implications

1. Starting body position must take into account relaxin affected joints.
2. Deter blood pressure rise by minimising isometric 'fixator' work.
3. Supine hypotensive syndrome.

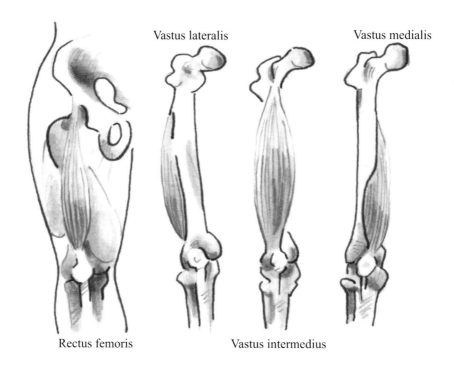

Vastus lateralis

Vastus medialis

Rectus femoris

Vastus intermedius

Figure 6.1: The quadriceps

Lower body exercises

Quadriceps: these are a group of muscles that form the thigh at the front of the body in the upper leg (see *Figure 6.1*). The muscles that make up the quadricep muscle group are:

- rectus femoris
- vastus lateralis
- vastus intermedius
- vastus medialis.

Origins and insertions

Rectus femoris   Origin: anterior inferior iliac spine (front of hip bone)
                     Inserts into the patella (knee bone) and tibia (lower leg bone)

Vastus lateralis   Origin: into top of femur on thigh bone
                     Inserts into knee bone and tibia

Vastus intermedius   Origin: into the upper two thirds of the femur or thigh bone
                     Inserts into the knee bone (patella) and tibia on lower leg

Vastus medialis   Origin: the head of the femur
                     Inserts into the patella (knee bone).

These muscles extend the leg by straightening the knee when running and walking. The quadriceps contraction helps slow you down and stabilises the body when coming to land after jumping. They also keep the knees straight when standing. The rectus femoris also flexes the hip.

Advantages of exercising

1. Strengthening of quadriceps aids in the ability to bend and lift effectively and correctly.
2. Walking is an excellent way of working aerobically while pregnant, minimising impact on relaxin affected joints. Strong quadriceps allows this to be performed effectively.
3. Stability of the knee joint is maintained, particularly by the vastus medialis. The increasing pressure of extra weight and potentially increased instability caused by relaxin hormone can be counteracted by exercising the quadriceps.
4. A 'natural overload' occurs as pregnancy progresses, because of the gradually increasing body weight (anything from two to four stone). Over a period of nine months, exercise ensures, in varying degrees, an increase in strength in quadriceps.

Leg exercises that contract the quadriceps muscle group include:

- half squats
- straight leg extensions.

Half squats

Position for exercising

1. Standing with or without support depending on which trimester of pregnancy has been reached and exercise ability of individual.
2. Feet should be hip distance apart, and pointing outward on the diagonal.
3. If using the support of a chair or wall, stand close enough to maintain a straight back while working.

Exercise technique and teaching points

1. Bend the knees into a half squat position with the back bent slightly forwards from the hips.
2. Do not take the knee joint beyond the range of the foot when in half squat position, try to keep in line.
3. Increased body weight and effect of relaxin on the knee joints can be exacerbated by squatting more deeply and taking the knee joint beyond the stability of the ankle joint.
4. Return to starting position by straightening knee joint. As the legs beocme straight and the knee extends, this is the contraction or work phase for the quadriceps. Work eigth to ten repetitions, then rest, work another muscle group, return and repeat. If feeling tired, do less, remember to listen to your body.

Half squats can be performed on dry land or in a pool environment. They can be incorporated into the warm-up session by mobilising hip joints, warming up muscle tissue and increasing pulse rate. They can also be utilised as linking moves in aerobic work and, of course, in the strength part of a fitness class.

Straight leg extensions

Position for exercising

1. Seated on a chair.
2. Ensure that the feet touch the floor. If of short stature, pack a lumbar support behind you, eg. rolled up towel or sweat shirt, to move you forward a little on your seat.
3. While working, to enhance stability, hold sides of chair under the seat, with one hand (on opposite side to working) or both hands if preferred. Chairs with arms can be used if available.

Exercise technique

1. Work one leg at a time, from right to left.
2. Lift one foot from the floor and straighten leg out in front until the knee is fully extended. This is the contraction phase of the exercise. The muscle fibres can be felt if a hand is placed on the 'bulking up' of the thigh while working.
3. Return the foot to the floor.
4. Try not to 'snap' the knee joint on full extension of the joint, keep the movement smooth and controlled, not jerky.
5. About eight to ten repetitions in one block, alternate legs, achievingtwo or three sets.

Trimester adaptions

* Land based class: this exercise should be performed only in a seated position by the pregnant woman. A standing posture is too demanding and unsafe. The changes in centre of gravity, distribution of bodyweight and changes in motor control all contribute to increasing instability and poor body control.
* Aqua adaptation: this exercise can be performed standing, in chest-deep water with 80% of the effect of gravity removed by the support of water and increased weightlessness, with some side rail support. Pace is an important consideration. Any exercise taught incorrectly is deemed controversial; a fast pace increases momentum and reduced control and quality of movement.

Hamstring curls

The hamstrings are collectively a group of muscles situated on the back of the upper thigh (see *Figure 6.2*). The individual muscles that make up this group are:

* semitendinosus
* semimembranosus
* biceps femoris.

Origins and insertions

All of the hamstring muscle group originate on the ischial tuberosity (the pelvic bones that are sat on). The semitendinosus and the semimembranosus muscle fibres insert into the tibia (lower leg bone, below the knee), while the biceps femoris inserts into the fibula, also in the lower leg.

Function

To flex or bend the knee and to extend the hip. When the knee is flexed, rotation of the knee can occur.

Position for exercise

Standing with support of a chair, wall, exercise barre, in pool holding the scum rail.

Exercise technique

With support, sweep one foot and leg backwards until toe is touching the floor. Bend knee of that leg and as flexion occurs try to touch the buttock with heel. This flexion phase of movements behind the body is when contraction of the hamstring muscle group occurs. Return foot to floor by extending and straightening knee.

Teaching points

1. Use a support, either the back of a chair, exercise rail or facing a wall.

2. Supporting leg should be soft at the knee joint, do not lock the knee joint out.

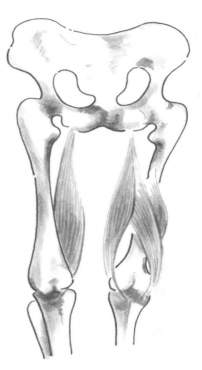

Figure 6.2: The hamstrings

3. If using wall or barre, face the support rather than sideways on, or stand directly behind a chair.

4. If using a chair make sure that it is the correct height for you. If necessary stack chairs so you are not leaning forward and creating further back and quadriceps strain on supporting leg.

5. Try to maintain a flat or even slightly rounded back as you work. Beware of 'hollowing' out the back as you work. If this occurs and you cannot maintain a flat back, stop exercising. Do only the number of repetitions that can be achieved with correct technique.

6. Try to incorporate 'resistance' as you work. Imagine a weight holding your foot on to the ground that you have to pull against to lift the foot towards the buttocks. This will enhance the effect of the exercise (see *Figure 6.3*).

Advantages of this exercise

1. Improving strength of the hamstrings aids the pregnant woman's ability to bend and lift with good technique, reducing stress on the vertebral column as pregnancy advances. As they work as antagonist to the quadriceps group both muscle groups should be exercised.

Figure 6.3: A hamstring curl

2. The hamstrings are instrumental in helping to maintain the correct pelvic tilt and therefore correct alignment between the pelvis and the spinal column, thus aiding good posture and helping to alleviate backache.

Trimester adaptations

More stable support is needed as pregnancy progresses. Repetitions may need to be decreased in the third trimester as increasing body weight and frontal 'load' make it more difficult to maintain correct body posture while exercising. Also, static contraction of quadriceps in the supporting leg is affected by increasing weight.

Aqua implications

1. Support of water lessens the effects of gravity, so exercise may feel easier to perform, even though resistance of water enhances the workload of the exercise.
2. Increased resistance of surrounding water will affect pace: choose music and rhythm that allow correct exercise technique.
3. Because of the effects of water surrounding the limb, when the foot is pushed back down from the buttock to the floor, the quadriceps muscle group is contracted, thus achieving a 'double work-out,' hamstring contraction as the knee flexes and the foot is brought up towards the buttock, and quadriceps contraction when the foot is returned to its starting position. This phenomenon occurs only in water, not in land based or dry site classes.

Toe 'pull ups' or 'foot lifts'

The muscle used for this exercise is the tibialis anterior. This muscle is situated on the front of the lower leg running longitudinally between the knee cap and ankle joint.

Origin

On the upper two thirds of the tibia.

Inserts

Into the inner surface of foot and first metatarsal (toe) bone.

Function

It is one of a group of muscles responsible for turning the foot inwards and producing movements that result in the top of the foot moving upwards towards the tibia bone at the front of the lower leg, 'plantar flexion'. It contracts strongly when standing on the outside of the foot.

Position for exercise

Seated on a chair, or on the floor, or standing in a pool. If using a chair ensure that both feet touch the floor. If not, use a lumbar support (towel or sweatshirt) to move the buttocks forward a little until this is achieved. If seated on the floor, place both hands behind and to the side as necessary to give support while working. It is tiring for back muscles to maintain an upright seated position especially in the last trimester of pregnancy. Provide plenty of opportunity to rest the back by leaning back on the hands between sets of repetitions.

Exercise technique

Seated on chair, pull the upper part of the foot up towards the lower leg flexing the ankle as this exercise is performed. Return the foot to the floor. This exercise can be performed with both feet together or alternate feet.

Seated on floor sit with legs straight out in front, hip distance apart. Pull the upper part of the foot up towards the tibia of the lower leg, flexing the ankle as this exercise is performed. Return the foot (feet) to starting position. Repeat eight to ten times, rest, rotate to different muscle group, return and repeat.

Teaching points

1. If standing ensure the feet are flat on the floor before starting.
2. Maintain smooth execution of the exercise, do not jerk the foot.

Advantages of exercising

It gives support to the long arch of the foot when the soles of the foot are turned inwards (inversion) and helps counteract 'flat feet'. The added weight of pregnancy and extra stress imposed on the ankle and foot can be counteracted by exercising the tibialis anterior muscle.

Aqua adaptations

Stand against the pool side with back to scum rail. Use hands each side to hold scum rail or pool rail. Bend supporting leg slightly at the knee, place other foot on the bottom of the pool, heel and toes touching the floor. Exercise in the same manner as if seated.

Side leg lifts

The muscles used during this exercise are the tensor faciae latae, gluteus medius and minimus (buttock muscles). The tensor faciae latae is attached to the anterior iliac spine (a protuberance of the hip bone) and runs laterally down the outside of the thigh, to a point about half way down the femur.

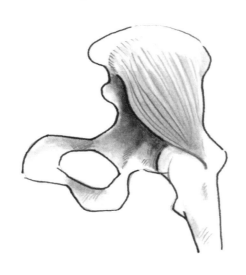

Origin

Anterior superior iliac spine.

Insertion

Inferior tibial tract (a strong tendon band on outside of thigh). Bends and abducts (moves from midline outwards) hip and straightens the knee joint.

Muscles also used during this exercise include:

- gluteus medius
  origin: outer surface of ilium
  insertion: greater trochanter
- gluteus minimus
  origin and insertion: as in 'medius' but beneath and behind (*see Figure 6.4*).

Figure 6.4: Gluteus medius

Positions for exercising

1. Standing with support eg. chair, wall, exercise barre.
2. Lying on floor on side.

Standing: exercise technique

Take weight on supporting leg, lift opposite leg out to the side and return to standing position.

Teaching points

1. Supporting leg should have a 'soft' knee joint. Do not lock out; aim for a small bend at knee on supporting leg.
2. Try to keep both hip joints in line as you lift leg out to the side, do not allow the hip joint opposite to the side that you are working to sag.
3. Keep the knee joint and quadriceps (thigh muscles at front of thigh), facing forward as you lift the leg out to the side.
4. Only a small lift is required to achieve muscle contraction. A high leg lift will create stress on the symphysis pubis joint at the front of the pelvis as the inside leg muscles are attached to this joint. As relaxin hormone has already affected the stability of the pelvic girdle and the increasing weight of the uterus (or womb) and its contents (baby, afterbirth and liquor), great care must be taken not to overexploit the extra flexibility created by relaxin hormone.
5. Lift the rib cage as you work, avoid 'slumping' on the opposite side.
6. Do approximately eight repetitions before changing side, avoid tiredness, especially in the last trimester (six to nine months) of pregnancy. Remember that static contractions of the thigh muscles take place in the supporting leg, while working the other. Pregnant women tire easily so ensure that support is available. Free standing should be avoided.

Lying on side

Ensure clean, warm, safe floor surface. Teach and observe the correct technique for pregnant women to get down safely on to floor or exercise mat.

Position for exercising

Adapt the position as you lie on the floor, bottom leg should be slightly bent with knee in front of body line. Top leg should be straight. Support head on hand with bent arm position. Upper arm and hand can be used to support by placing hand on floor in front of chest.

Exercise technique

Lift straight leg up, then lower back down to starting position.

Teaching points

1. Keep the hips rolled forward in the side lying position. This is easier to do when pregnant as the weight of the baby makes this easier than when non-pregnant.
2. Do not lift the leg too high as this creates stress on the symphysis pubis joint.
3. Do not turn the leg outward as you lift, keep thigh and knee joint facing wall in front of you as you lift, in order to achieve contraction in the muscle groups being targeted.

4. Rest when you need to. Do approximately eight repetitions, remember to listen to your body; if you feel tired do less. If you want to do more, rotate to a different muscle group, then come back and work the exercise again, rather than overloading with too many repetitions.

Advantages of this exercise

1. Helps strengthen leg and gluteal muscles to aid pregnant women in correct bending and lifting technique.
2. Helps in maintaining pelvic stability.

Trimester adaptations

When lying on your side a less straight body line may be used. As pregnancy progresses and fundal height load increases, it becomes more difficult to achieve a straight body line. This makes it easier for lordosis (extra lumbar curvature) to occur, causing further strain on lower back. By bending the knees forward in front of the body line, greater balance and less chance of increasing further lordosis is achieved.

Aqua implications

1. Extra resistance by surrounding water enhance the exercise.
2. Support of the body gives less work for the supporting leg, so more repetitions may be achieved in comfort in water based class.
3. The pace of the exercise will need to take into account the resistance offered by water around the limb. If using music, check that the timing of the beat that you are working to is appropriate; can the exercise be performed with good technique at that speed? Remember, safety is all important.

Heel raises

The gastrocnemius and soleus muscles are used during this movement. They are situated in the lower legs and form part of the calf musculature.

Origins and insertions

The gastrocnemius originates above the knee joint on the lower end of the femur in two places. It inserts into the Achilles tendon at the back of the heel.

The soleus originates on the upper two thirds of the tibia and fibula. It inserts into the Achilles tendon at the back of the heel (see *Figure 6.5*).

Function

The gastrocnemius is used to propel the body forward and upwards when running, jumping, hopping and skipping. Heel raising exercises with the knees fully attended or 'locked out' will effectively exercise and strengthen gastrochemius.

The soleus is one of the most important plantar flexors (movement of the ankle and foot away from the tibia) of the ankle, as is the gastrocnemius. This is especially effective when the knees are slightly bent. Any movement with body weight on the foot with the knee flexed or extended produces contraction of the soleus muscle. Running, jumping, hopping, skipping and dancing activate the soleus.

Position for exercise

Stand with support, eg. using chair, wall, exercise rail, scum rail in pool. Safety may be compromised by using another person or exercise partner as your 'support' because they will be as unstable as the pregnant woman, stability cannot be ensured. A 'fixed' support is more desirable.

Exercise technique

1. Stand with feet hip distance apart, toes pointing forward, feet flat on floor.
2. If using a chair as a support, ensure that the back rail is the correct height for the participant. If necessary 'stack' the chair to ensure a straight back while working.
3. Raise heels together from the floor, lower and return to starting position.

Teaching points

1. Use double heel raises if working on land. The added weight gain of pregnancy, increased clumsiness and reduced stability of the ankle joint caused by relaxin hormone, decrease control and performance. Single heel raises on land increase the risk of turning the ankle over. Double heel raises increase stability.

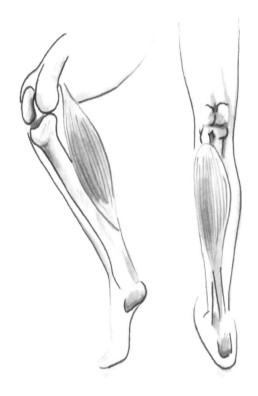

Figure 6.5: Gastrocnemius and soleus muscles

2. Try not to roll the ankle outwards as the heels are lifted from the ground. Do only the amount of repetitions that can be performed with good technique.
3. On returning the heels to the ground, do not 'lift' the toes off the supporting surface, keep them firmly planted on the ground.

Aqua implications

The deeper the water, the more support and less effect of gravity. To increase a gentle 'overload' effect single heel raises can be performed in a water based class by tucking one foot behind the lower calf of the opposite leg before lifting up the opposite heel. Make sure that a support (scum rail or pool side) is utilised while working.

Advantages of this exercise

1. Mobility of the ankle joint, achieved by the action of gastrocnemius and soleus helps maintain general mobility of walking or performing exercise routines using the legs, in ante- and postnatal exercise classes.

2. Physiological oedema, or swelling, in the ankles, especially in the last trimester can be alleviated by maintaining mobility.

3. The 'natural pump' effect of these muscles, when contracting, can aid in maintaining venous return from the calf back to the heart, thus minimising the risk of varicose veins and improving blood flow.

Upper body exercises

These exercises include:

- press-ups
- triceps extension
- lateral pulls
- trapezius squeezes.

Press-ups

The pectoralis major muscle, which is used during this exercise, is situated on the anterior (front) surface of the chest wall, either side of the sternum (or breastbone), filling the space of the chest region between the shoulder girdle and the sixth rib.

Origins

Upper fibres into the shoulder girdle (or clavicle) lower fibres into the front of the first six ribs and the sternum of that area.

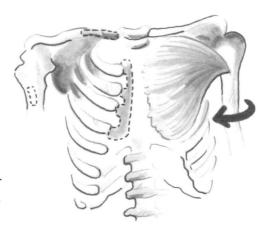

Figure 6.6: Pectoralis major

Insertion

Into a flat tendon 2–3" wide into a groove of the humerus bone in the upper arm (see *Figure 6.6*).

Function

1. When the arm (or arms) is held in the horizontal position, this muscle draws the arms across, towards the chest midline.

2. When the arm is away from the body (abducted), pectoralis major moves the arm down towards the body.

3. It is also responsible for internally rotating the humerus bone in the upper arm in towards the body.

Position for exercise

Seated on a chair or on the floor, standing either on land or water based. In box position, on your hands and knees on the floor.

Exercise technique

Seated or standing: take both arms, bent at the elbow, hands uppermost, upper arm level with the shoulders, out to either side of the body. Using this as the starting position, keeping the arms bent, draw them both inwards across the body, to meet in the midline, return to standing position.

Box position:

1. Use correct technique to get down on to your hands and knees on to an exercise mat, towel or carpeted surface.
2. In the hands and knees position take nose down towards floor between hands, bending the arms on descent and straightening the arms on return.

Teaching points

Seated or standing:

1. Keep the movement smooth and fluid, do not jerk.
2. Try not to drop the elbows as you work.
3. Be aware of the fixator muscle groups on the shoulder that will be in a state of static or fixed contraction in order to support the arms while working. Excessive numbers of repetitions will cause discomfort in the shoulder region, in the deltoid muscles.
4. When returning the arms from midline back to starting position, do not fling, as the momentum caused by this poor technique reduces safety and effectiveness.
5. If seated on the floor, ensure plenty of rest periods for the back and erector spine muscles by allowing opportunity to lean back on hands.
6. Standing position can be tiring in the second and third trimesters if performed on a dry site. More support and ease of working position is achieved if performed standing in chest-deep water.
7. If standing, ensure feet are flat, toes pointing forward, hip distance apart.
8. Ensure that the knee joint is soft and not locked out allowing a correct pelvic tilt to be achieved while working.

Box position:

1. Ensure that hands are directly in line with the shoulders and knees in line with the hips when on hands and knees.
2. It is vital that a flat back is maintained throughout working. Stop if sagging or 'hollowing out' occurs while working. Either correct the technique, have a rest, or reduce the amount of repetitions being performed.
3. Ensure that the elbow joint is not 'snapped back' when returning to the straight arm position. To avoid this potential trauma to the elbow joint ensure a slight bend (or softness) in the elbow joint when commencing and on return to starting position.
4. This exercise can be made to feel easier or more difficult if the nose is placed in front of the hand line. If behind the hand line it is easier. Aim to work in line with the hands on the descent phase.
5. Because of the destabilising effect of relaxin hormone on joints and the increasing weight of pregnancy, extended press-ups, where the knees are moved further back out of line with the hips or straight legs are extended out behind, are contraindicated after about 14 weeks of

pregnancy. Relaxin hormone is at its highest level at this stage of pregnancy and this level will be maintained until after delivery.

6. Choose an appropriate pace that will allow the exercise to be performed with good technique. There is an increased risk of injury if the exercise is performed too fast, with poor technique. If performed too slowly the demands of this exercise are greatly increased and the effort required is demanding and potentially tiring for most pregnant women.

Aqua implications

1. The added support of chest-deep water allows the standing position to be used with less risk of tiredness.
2. The resistance created by surrounding water enhances the effect of the exercise.
3. Because of the surrounding aquatic environment, the pace will need to be adjusted to allow correct technique.
4. Resistance is added by surrounding water but can be enhanced further. As the arms are brought together across the chest, imagine that you are having to squeeze a thick pad of foam in between them, relax as you release and move arms back to standing position.
5. Use hand paddles, blow up arm bands, or webbed gloves to increase resistance.
6. Standing in front of the scum rail, feet hip distance apart, hold the scum rail with both hands, lean into the pool side, bending the elbows, then push back to starting position. This works the pectoralis major muscles.

Advantages of this exercise

The following advantages result from press-ups:

* Improved function in ability to lift and carry, an advantage called upon many times not only antenatally, but also in the postnatal period.
* Muscle tone is improved giving extra support to breast tissue.
* Both smaller and larger breasts benefit, giving an improved shape to the breast.
* Blood supply to the breast area is increased. Some authorities suggest an improvement in lactation, as prolactin levels, (one of the hormones responsible for lactation) are elevated in the regular exerciser.

Triceps extensions

The triceps brachii muscle is situated on the back of the upper arm and is responsible (with the help of another muscle called the anconeus) for extending or straightening the elbow.

Origin

Muscle fibres originate on the scapula (shoulder girdle) and on two separate sections of the humerus bone.

Insertion

All fibres insert into the ulna, a bone in the lower part of the arm, below the elbow joint (see *Figure 6.7*).

Function

Triceps brachii is involved in movements that strengthen the elbow joint such as pushing movements and hand balancing. Some muscle fibres that originate on the scapula are responsible also for extension of the shoulder joint.

Position for exercise

Standing or seated.

Exercise technique

With slightly bent arms and a loose fist, place the upper arms into close contact with the body and slide the elbows back until they are behind the body. It is important to keep the upper arms in place, straighten the arm by sweeping the hands backwards and return to starting position by flexing at the elbow joint.

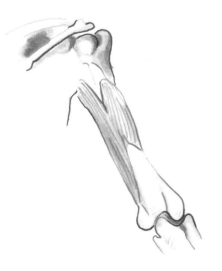

Figure 6.7: Triceps brachii

Variations in technique: work triceps brachii by clasping both hands above the head, with bent elbows. Straightening the arms in this position will also contract triceps brachii muscle. Minimise repetitions in this position due to potential rise in blood pressure.

Teaching points

Keep shoulders relaxed, do not tense. Ensure that the hands are in a loose fist only. Do not snap the elbow joint as you extend the lower arms back, as this will stress the elbow joint. If seated on a chair (ensure no arms on chair), work one side at a time, using other hand to hold side of chair for support, in order to add some variety, or work both sides together.

Aqua implications

Exercise effect enhanced by performing triceps extensions in chest-deep water due to resistance of water around limbs. Further resistance can be incorporated by holding partially blown up arm bands or webbed gloves. Experiment yourself to find out what is comfortable for you as the workload can be dramatically increased. The pace of the exercise needs to be slowed down accordingly to ensure safe effective technique.

Advantages of this exercise

Pushing activities, such as prams and pushchairs, and carrying and balancing activities, such as when travelling with your baby or toddler (ie. carrying changing bags, shopping, baby) are better coped with and performed with greater ease if the triceps brachii is well toned or exercised.

Lateral pulls

The latissimus dorsi muscle is situated either side of the spinal column, on the back, from the lower six thoracic vertebrae (T6 to T12), from the lowest three ribs, down to the lumbar region of the spine and the sacrum (the flat bone at the back of the pelvis).

Origin

Muscle fibres originate on the iliac crest (part of the hipbone that juts out at the sides), the back of the sacrum, the lumbar and thoracic vertebrae and the lowest three ribs.

Insertion

Into the intertubercular groove of the humerus bone in the upper arm, just below the arm pit (see *Figure 6.8*).

Function

To pull the abducted arm down to the side and towards the midline of the body; exercises in which the arms are pulled down such as rope climbing, dips on parallel bars, rowing and pulling a bar on weights down towards the shoulders (known as lat pulls) will contract latissimus dorsi muscle.

Position for exercise

Free standing, or side standing with support (eg. exercise barre) or sitting on a chair. In chest-deep water in swimming pool.

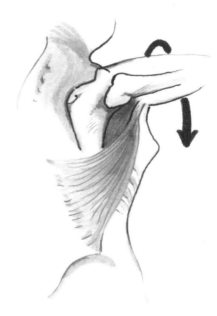

Figure 6.8: Latissimus dorsi

Exercise technique

If standing, ensure correct posture. Raise both arms above the head, grasp an imaginary rail, pull down the arms aiming to pull the imaginary rail down behind the head towards the shoulders. Return both arms to starting position, ie. raised above the head.

Teaching Points

1. Maintain anterior pelvic tilt, try to reduce lumbar lordosis if standing.
2. Imagine there is resistance on the barre above the head, squeeze and pull down to enhance the effects of the exercise.
3. Keep the movement smooth, release and relax as arms are returned above the head.
4. Minimise repetitions to eight to ten as prolonged arm raising can effect blood pressure and instigate a rise in blood pressure.
5. If seated on a chair, make sure that there are no chair arms, as they inhibit performance of the exercise and bruise the elbows.

Aqua implications

Can be performed in the more supportive environment of a swimming pool. For interest, add squat side steps in time with lateral pulls for variety and to maintain muscle activity and warmth if pool is cooler than optimum.

Advantages of this exercise

This muscle is one of the most important extensor muscles (to extend, to straighten) of the humerus (in the upper arm) and is also responsible for moving the arm horizontally, away from the chest. Its interplay with other muscle groups ensures effective pulling and lifting movements.

Trapezius squeezes

The trapezius is situated either side of the spinal column in the cervical and thoracic areas on the back extending up into the base of the skull and out to the sides of the clavicle and scapula (bony shoulder girdle).

Origin

The muscle fibres originate on the base of the skull, cervical vertebrae and thoracic vertebrae.

Insertion

Into the clavicle and scapula which are the two bones involved in movement of the shoulders. They usually act together as one unit (see *Figure 6.9*).

Function

The trapezius muscle is responsible for pulling upwards and raising arms above the head. When arms are held out at the side of the body, the trapezius fixes the scapula in place and allows this to happen. When lifting with the hands (eg. heavy bags) the trapezius contracts. Also carrying baby or heavy objects on the edge of the shoulder contracts thetrapezius muscle.

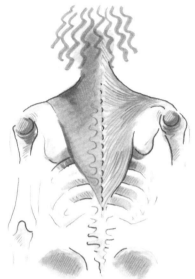

Figure 6.9: Trapezius

Position for exercise

Standing on a dry site or in the water. Sitting on a chair or on the floor.

Exercise technique

Standing:

1. Raise arms, with bent elbows, to front of body, upper arms level with shoulders. Push shoulders backwards, drawing shoulder blades closer together on the upper back. While pulling elbows towards the back of the body, trying not to drop the elbows as you work, return to starting position.

2. Take both arms above the head. Imagine you are grasping a 'rail' above your head. The action of taking the arms above your head and pulling down the imaginary rail behind your head towards your shoulders contracts the trapezius and will activate latissimus dorsi muscle.

3. If standing when performing either exercise think about maintaining correct posture throughout, feet hip distance apart, do not lock knee joints, avoid excessive lumbar lordosis by

tucking bottom in and trying to maintain a pelvic tilt that does not stress the lumbar region of the spine.

Sitting:

If seated, ensure that feet touch the floor. If they don't, tuck a rolled up towel or sweatshirt behind you to bring your bottom further forward on the chair.

Teaching points

Be aware that static contraction of the deltoid muscle on the tops of the shoulders will occur, as they are responsible for holding up the arms at shoulder level. Plan the number of repetitions to be performed accordingly. Keep the action smooth, do not jerk. Do not drop the elbows as you work. Remember that the slower the pace, the longer the deltoid muscle has to statically contract. Too fast a pace will compromise safe, effective technique. If seated on a chair, either side can be worked separately by holding on to the chair with one hand for extra support, and working the trapezius on the other side. This may be more comfortable and less tiring for the non regular exerciser and women in the third trimester. If seated on the floor, give ample opportunity to lean back on to hands in order to rest the back muscles (erector spinae). Keep repetitions down to eight to ten, rotating onto another muscle group, then returning to repeat the exercise.

Aqua implications

Performing trapezius squeezes in chest-deep water will enhance the exercise, because of the resistance of the water around the limbs and torso. Women in the third trimester of pregnancy may find it more supportive and comfortable to stand in chest-deep water. Standing sideways on, by the side of the pool, using the scum rail for support, one side of the body can be exercised at a time, giving variety and more scope to choreograph your routine, if using music as a motivator.

Shoulder 'shrugging' will also contract the trapezius muscle. Seated or standing, arms loose by the sides of the body, lift both shoulders up, towards the ears, then release to standing position. For variety, lift and raise alternate shoulders, or lift right, lift left, lower right, lower left in time to appropriately paced music to add variety and enjoyment to your exercise routine.

Advantages of this exercise

Well-toned trapezius muscles will help to ease the stress of lifting and carrying. New parents will be activating this muscle not only by carrying an increasingly heavier weight, namely the baby, but also by the lifting and carrying tasks involving equipment, eg. prams, pushchairs, changing bags and all the paraphernalia that goes with having a baby and quite soon a toddler. Lifting and carrying children and pushchairs on and off buses, or in and out of the car, up and down escalators can be exhausting. Cope more efficiently by regularly exercising the trapezius muscle.

The abdominal muscles

This section will cover:
- origins and insertions of muscles
- functions

- advantages of exercising
- implications of pregnancy
- position to exercise
- exercise technique
- teaching points
- contraindications
- postnatal considerations.

The area of the body that usually concerns most women before, during and definitely after pregnancy is the abdominal corset, or stomach area. Much emphasis is placed on having a flat stomach as this is seen to be sexy, attractive and vitally important in order to be the fashionable norm of size 10 or less. This, of course, is not the norm for most of us, although we are brainwashed into thinking that it is. The physiological process of being pregnant, giving birth and the associated changes that the body must adapt to and slowly reverse in the postnatal period, not only dramatically changes a woman's physical shape but alters her own perceptions about body and self. The changing shape of a woman's body during pregnancy is often seen by a certain sector of society as less than desirable; women may perceive themselves as less than perfect, instead of adopting the stance that an absolute miracle of creation is occurring within their bodies. Common sense tells us that 'something has to give, somewhere' in order to accommodate the growing baby and the body sensibly adapts as rectus abdominis, two halves of muscle fibre held together midline by fascia, begins to separate midline in order for this to happen. I have devoted a whole section to the abdominal muscles as they play such an important role in protecting the spine. Mothers will be bending and lifting continually for at least a few years. Correct technique and the vital role that the abdominal corset plays cannot be emphasised enough.

The abdominal muscles fill the gap between the ribs and pelvis, and form a natural elastic corset. Collectively the muscles consist of rectus abdominis (see *Figure 6.10*); internal obliques (see *Figure 6.11*); external obliques (see *Figure 6.12*); transverse abdominis (see *Figure 6.13*); and quadratus lumborum (see *Figure 6.14*).

Functions

1. They act as a protective splint for the spine.
2. They help to maintain the correct pelvic tilt and re-align the pelvis with the spine.
3. They support and protect the abdominal contents.
4. They allow and produce controlled movements.
5. They provide support for the pregnant uterus.
6. They aid expulsive movements such as coughing.

Vomiting, defecation and pushing during the process of childbirth during the second stage of labour when the transverse abdominals act as secondary powers to help the contracting uterus push out and expel the baby along the birth canal, all utilise the contraction of abdominal corset muscles.

Rectus abdominis

Origin

On the front of the pubic bone, at the front midline of the pelvis.

Insertion

Into the fifth, sixth and seventh rib and the xiphoid process (the bony protuberance between the ribcage on the front of the chest). Some muscles in this area of the body are different in that they are not attached from bone to bone, as in the rest of the body, but attach to fascia (or aponeurosis), a fibrous membrane that covers, supports and connects. There are such connections of fascia within the rectus abdominis area.

Function

The rectus abdominis muscle is responsible for flexion in the lumbar region. The tilt of the pelvis is controlled by the rectus

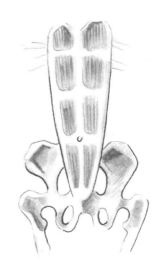

Figure 6.10: Rectus abdominis

abdominis. Flattening of the lumbar (or lower back) region is achieved by pelvic tilting or 'lifting the pelvis up in front' by contracting the rectus abdominis muscle.

Internal oblique muscles

Origin

Muscle fibres originate on the iliac crest, at the front of the pelvis, the inguinal ligament, and each side at the front of the pelvis and lumbar fascia.

Insertion

Cartilage of the 8th, 9th and 10th ribs and the linea alba. Before pregnancy the linea alba can be seen as a white line running downwards from the navel towards the symphysis pubis at the front up to the pelvis. During pregnancy extra pigmentation causes this line to turn brown, when it is then known as the linea negra (or brown line).

Function

Contraction of internal oblique muscles, on either side of the torso, brings about lumbar flexion and lateral (sideways) flexion

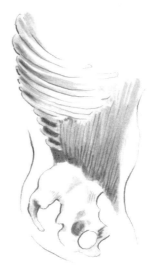

Figure 6.11: Internal obliques

to the right or left; contraction of the right side causes lateral flexion to the right and of the left to the left side. Muscle fibres run diagonally in a direction opposite to that of the external oblique muscle fibres when lateral flexion occurs; the internal oblique and external oblique muscles always work on opposite sides to each other and together to produce the lateral or sideways flexion.

External oblique muscles

Origin

Muscle fibres originate on the borders of the lower eight ribs at the side of the chest.

Insertion

Into the iliac crest (the top of the flared out portion of the hip bone) the inguinal ligament of the front of the pelvis and fascia of the rectus abdominis muscle.

Function

Situated on each side of the trunk, these muscles aid rotation (or twisting) of the torso, working separately on each side. When the trunk rotates to the right, the left external oblique muscles contracts, and vice versa.

Figure 6.12: External obliques

Transverse abdominis muscles

Origin

Attached to the iliac crest at the front of the pelvis, the inguinal ligament, inner surface of the lowest six ribs and lumbar fascia.

Insertion

Into the crest of the pubis, into the ileopectineal line (a point of reference on the front of the pelvis) and into the abdominal aponeurosis to the linea alba.

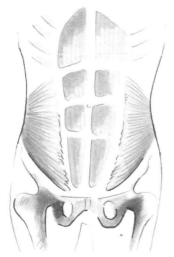

Figure 6.13:Transverse abdominis

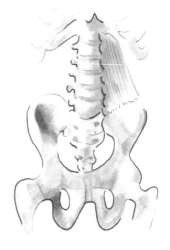

Figure 6.14: Quadratus lumborum

Function

This muscle helps hold the abdomen flat, with help from the rectus abdominis and the internal and external obliques. Forced exhalation uses contraction of the transverse abdominis by 'sucking in' the abdomen and attempting to pull the abdominal contents in as close to the spine as possible. This can be performed sitting, standing or lying.

Changes in the abdominal muscles during pregnancy

At 12 weeks gestation the uterus becomes an abdominal organ, instead of a pelvic one. Further growth in weight and dimension ensures that eventually it will lean forward on to the abdominal corset and separation midline of the rectus abdominis muscle will occur along the fascial sheath. Obviously, this allows more room for the enlarging uterus or womb. Multiple pregnancies (twins, triplets) very large babies and repeated, frequent pregnancies will take their toll on the tone, elasticity and strength of the abdominal muscles. Pre-pregnancy tone will also affect to what degree separation occurs. Each woman and each pregnancy will affect the abdominal muscles in a different way. For this reason it is impossible to give a carte blanche prescription of exercise such as a 'six week postnatal deadline' to introduce abdominal curls. Each woman should be assessed individually postnatally as to what her workload abdominally at that stage should be.

Some concerns about the supine position

Some authorities believe that performing abdominal curls lying flat, using the upper body as a weight or resistance to lift the head and shoulders off the floor are acceptable after 16 weeks of pregnancy and do not constitute a hazard. My concerns are that when lifting the head and shoulders, the pregnant uterus is pressed against the separate halves of the rectus abdominis, creating more trauma and maybe further widening the gap for the muscle fibre, which has been thinned and stretched over the pregnant uterus, from 11" pre-pregnancy to 20" or more, and that it is likely to contract in two halves, instead of in one unit. Lying flat on a surface to perform abdominal curls also risks inducing supine hypotensive syndrome.

Position for abdominal curls

Prior to the 16th week of pregnancy, lying on the back on the floor to perform abdominal curls is not considered to be detrimental as the pregnant uterus and its contents are not large enough to cause supine hypotensive syndrome. Supine hypotensive syndrome (supine = lying flat, hypotensive = low blood pressure) occurs when a pregnant uterus falls back into large blood vessels returning blood back to the heart. Blood flow is impeded, cardiac output reduced and blood pressure falls, causing dizziness and faintness. For this reason, pregnant women should not be encouraged to lie flat on their backs after the 16th week of pregnancy. If less than 16 weeks pregnant, abdominal curls can be performed in the following position:

up to 16 weeks gestation:	lie flat, knees bent, feet flat on the floor hip distance apart.
if more than 16 weeks gestation:	keeping the knees relaxed stand with the feet hip distance apart. Sit on chair, or sit on floor or in box position on hands and knees.
postnatal exercise:	position for exercising will depend on the degree of separation of rectus abdominis and type of delivery but lying flat on the floor is now not hazardous.

Exercise technique

Abdominal curls (before 16 weeks gestation or postnatally if rectus abdominis gap less than two finger width).

1. Lie flat, knees bent, feet hip distance apart.
2. Place hands on either side of abdomen.
3. Breathe in, flattening abdomen and push the small of the back onto the floor.
4. Breathe out, keeping abdomen as flat as possible, lift head and shoulders as far as able. Do not sit up as this is not necessary as the abdominal muscles do not work after 45% of lift. It is the powerful hip flexors that then become the prime mover in achieving the 'sit up' position.
5. As you breath in, in a controlled manner return head and shoulders back to starting position, ready to repeat (see *Figure 6.15*).

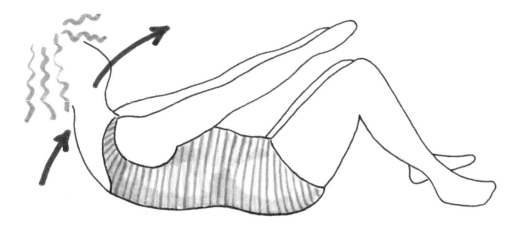

Figure 6.15: Abdominal curl

Teaching points

1. Ensure knees are bent, do not work with straight legs.
2. Do not tuck feet under a support while working. Maintain stability through body's own ability and strength to dictate what you can achieve comfortably.

3. Observe for 'doming' of abdominal muscle while working. Try to eliminate this by maintaining a flat abdomen throughout. Persistent doming indicates either poor technique, a need to reduce workload or use of a less demanding exercise for the abdominal corset, eg. static abdominal contractions, eliminating the use of the body's weight as a resistor.
4. Maintain slight pelvic tilt and ensure lumbar region remains flat on the floor while working.
5. Workload can be increased during the postnatal period by lengthening the length of the lever.

Exercise after 16 weeks gestation — static abdominal contraction

Positions for exercising

Standing, sitting, in box position on the hands and knees.

Standing technique

1. Feet hip distance apart.
2. Knees soft, toes pointed forwards.
3. Hips in line.
3. Ribcage lifted.
4. Place hands on abdomen, either side of the baby and breathe in.
5. On exhalation, contract abdominal muscles, tuck bottom under and tilt pelvis slightly backwards. (Think of trying to bring the symphysis pubis bone at the front of the bony pelvis in towards the baby.) Remember the three Ts, tuck, tilt and tighten, contracting the abdominal muscles around the baby as you tilt. Hold for a few seconds.
6. Breathe in as you release to starting position.

Teaching points

1. When releasing to starting position beware of increasing the lumbar curve in the lower back, do not 'kick out' the bottom, release to midline only.
2. Perform in a smooth, controlled movement. The lower back is vulnerable, especially during pregnancy, and injury and fast repetitions may be detrimental.
3. Observe your technique by standing sideways on in front of a mirror, if you can. As you tuck, tilt and tighten, see how your baby in the uterus/womb is lifted up and tucked in closer to your body as you perform static abdominal contraction.
4. Do not lock out the knee joints. Ensure that they remain 'soft' throughout.
5. Eight repetitions equals a set, rest or rotate to another muscle group. Return and repeat.

Benefits of this exercise

Backache can be reduced. The static abdominal contraction, or pelvic tilting, play an important role in maintaining the stability and position of the pelvis and its interplay with the spine. Poor abdominal tone and weak stretched musles from frequent or multiple pregnancies are instrumental in causing avoidable stress on the back and spine, especially the lumbar region; some backache of pregnancy is undoubtedly exacerbated by poor abdominal tone. By holding the pelvis up, rectus abdominis muscles help to flatten the back and reduce the lumbar curve. Ideally, the abdominal corset should be well-toned and strong before pregnancy and back strengthening exercises should form an integral part of your exercise routine before and after delivery. The abdomen is for many women the part of the body that most attention is paid to and achieving a flat stomach and keeping it that way supersedes the need to strengthen back musculature. Fear of a protruding abdomen, illogical though that may be during pregnancy, drives many women to continue performing abdominal curls throughout pregnancy in ever increasing repetitions. The teacher should confirm the benefits of pelvic tilting and reassure the pregnant woman that abdominal tone can be maintained without repetitive, frequent abdominal curls.

Seated technique

1. Ensure that the chair is the correct height, feet flat on the ground, back in contact with the chair or a firm support, eg. pillow, cushion, rolled up sweatshirt etc. in place behind lumbar region or lower back.
2. If feet do not touch the ground flat, move further forward on the seat and tuck a rolled up towel or support behind you.
3. Place hands on either side of the abdomen, the same technique as for standing position. Sit erect in the chair for support. As you breathe out and contract the abdominal muscles, push the small of the back into the chair. Hold the contraction for a few seconds before releasing as you inhale, ready to repeat.
4. Perform one set or 8 repetitions, rest or rotate to different muscle group, then repeat again.

Teaching points

These are as for the standing position. As this is a more supported position it is less tiring and appropriate for the second and third trimesters of pregnancy.

Box position (on the hands and knees)

1. On the hands and knees, make sure that hands are directly under shoulders and pointing forwards, do not lock elbow joints. Knees should be directly in line with hips, knees hip distance apart.
2. A flat back must be maintained at all times, do not 'hollow out' in the middle.

Exercise technique

1. Breathe in, as you exhale tuck, tilt and tighten. Tuck the seat underneath, tilt the pelvis in towards the baby and your body and tighten the abdominal muscles, pulling inwards and breathing out.
2. Hold the contraction for a few seconds.
3. Breathe in as you release and return to starting position.

Teaching points

1. Do not allow the back to hollow out, maintain a straight back throughout.
2. Do not hold the contraction of abdominal muscles for any longer than a few seconds. Breath holding will cause a rise in blood pressure if prolonged and can create the Valsalva effect, causing faintness and dizziness.

3. Do eight repetitions, then rest by leaning back on to heels and lower legs. Remember the increased weight of the body onto arms and shoulders will need to be relieved regularly between sets of exercise.

4. This position may not be appropriate if carpal tunnel syndrome is present in the wrist and hand.

Contraindications to exercises for the abdominal muscles

1. After 16 weeks of pregnancy do not perform abdominal curls or 'crunches'.

2. Do not perform straight leg sit ups at any time before, during or after pregnancy. The hip flexor muscles generate great force in this position and often cause arching of the lumbar region in the lower back.

3. If a gap of more than two fingers width is present between the two halves of the rectus abdominis antenatally and postnatally do not use resistance (ie. weight of baby) to work abdominals. Use static contraction (or isometric contraction) instead.

4. Wrapping hands around opposite sides of abdomen before lifting head and shoulders does not protect or make an abdominal curl any safer to perform in 2nd or 3rd trimester, as stretched, weakened, separated muscle corset will still have to try to contract over a 'hill' (or your uterus with baby in it). Muscles can only pull, not push and nowhere in the body are muscle fibres expected to contract in anything but a straight line.

5. The weight of multiple pregnancies may be too great a strain on the musculature of the back and a seated position may be more comfortable and safer, except for the 1st trimester.

6. If you cannot maintain a flat back while working in this position, opt for a standing or seated position, to ensure safe technique and reduce excess strain on the back.

7. If you have a diagnosed back injury, past or present, always consult your midwife, physiotherapist or GP prior to commencing exercise regimes of any sort.

Postnatal exercises for the abdominals

Immediately after delivery

Most mothers are aware as they hold their baby for the first time that the deceptively taut large abdomen may have suddenly changed into a quivering soft mass of toneless tissue that looks as if it will never be the same again. Excess weight gained during pregnancy which has been deposited over the abdomen suddenly becomes painfully obvious. At what stage should a newly delivered mother start to exercise her abdominal muscles again? Which exercises are appropriate in those first few early weeks following delivery?

The first two weeks postpartum

Most women are physically and mentally overwhelmed by the experience of giving birth. Some will have had an easy labour that lasted only a few short hours, others will have endured longer labours, that may have included instrumental deliveries using forceps, ventouse, or Caesarean sections. The first couple of nights will often be sleepless due to the demands of the baby, a busy hospital environment and the excitement of visitors and family alike celebrating the birth of the baby. The huge physiological adaptations that take place within the body following delivery, lack of sleep, adaptation to the new role of mother and parent, physical traumas such as perineal or abdominal stitches, breasts full of milk and swinging mood changes associated with massive drops of hormone levels all contribute to a feeling of exhaustion for many women in those first few weeks. If parents have had little or no sleep then it seems sensible to curtail how much exercise is participated in. Remember that the pregnant body changed and adapted over a nine month period, do not expect it suddenly to revert to its previous shape, size and tone in a few short weeks.

Abdominal exercise two weeks postpartum

This is a good time to check for separation of the rectus abdominis muscle and assess the width of the gap. Refer to the section under the heading 'Rectus abdominis' to illustrate how to do this. Remember if more than a two finger width gap (longitudinally) is present, resistance work is prohibited at this stage. Static abdominal contraction and pelvic tilting are excellent exercises, if performed with correct technique, that will contribute greatly to improving tone to the abdominal corset.

Postnatal variations of the abdominal curl

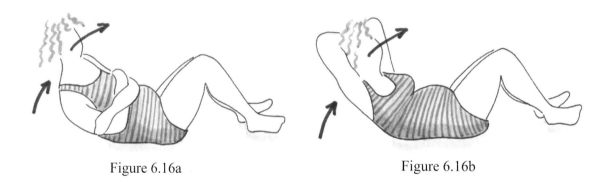

Figure 6.16a   Figure 6.16b

1. Lying flat, hands placed on top of thighs, slide hands up towards knees while performing abdominal curl. Slide back to starting position.
2. Cross arms across chest, slightly increasing weight to be lifted, keep in this position while working, thus increasing resistance (see *Figure 6.16a*).
3. Place hands either side of head, elbows out. Do not grasp or pull on head while working. Maintain fingertip touch only throughout. Longer body lever enhances exercise (see *Figure 6.16b*).

Static abdominal contractions/pelvic tilts

A firm bed or floor is an ideal support for recommencing pelvic tilting, as practised throughout your pregnancy. Now that the baby is extra uterine, lying flat will not create the problems that it would have if you were still pregnant. Many hospital beds are too soft but some worthwhile, gentle pelvic tilting can be performed, at your own pace if you are bed bound. If you are mobile, standing or seated positions can be utilised to perform pelvic tilts.

Position for exercise

Lie on a firm surface either on a bed or the floor with the knees bent, feet hip distance apart, hands placed either side on abdomen.

Exercise technique

Breathe in, as you exhale push the small of the back down towards the floor or bed, tighten the abdominal muscles pulling them in. You should feel the pelvis 'tip' backwards, as the symphysis pubis joint at the front of the pelvis lifts a little up towards the rib cage. Hold this tightening for a few seconds, and as you release breathe in, ready to repeat again.

Teaching points

1. Remember to breathe out on the 'exertion phase' of the exercise, ie. as you tighten and pull in the abdomen.
2. As you flatten the lower back, think about reducing the gap between the lumbar region of the spine and the support surface. Place a hand underneath in the lumbar region and try to squeeze against it with your back.
3. Because of the stretch imposed and the lengthening of rectus abdominis muscles, many women complain of feeling nothing as they contract and pull in the abdomen. By placing hands on the abdomen, the 'tightening' effect can be more easily felt and reinforces the feeling that the muscle still has a little tone.
4. Remember the three T's, tuck, tilt and tighten.
5. Perform six to eight repetitions if you can, less if tired. Repeat three to four times a day if your baby allows it.

Abdominal exercises following Caesarean section

Although the skin, fat and fascia are cut through when a Caesarean section is performed, usually the rectus abdominis muscle (already separated midline at the fascial sheath; see the later section under the heading 'rectus abdominis') is pulled apart, to expose the uterus or womb, by the obstetrician. The muscle layer is not usually cut through or incised. Some surgeons will put a few stitches into the two halves of the rectus abdominis following birth, when resuturing, others do not. Static abdominal contractions (or pelvic tilting) can be performed soon after delivery, depending very much on discomfort levels, the healing process and the condition of each individual woman. Often two weeks following delivery by Caesarean many scars are externally healed, with sutures being removed around the sixth day following delivery. If there is any delay in the healing process, pain or inflammation of any sort, or any discharge from the scar, specific advice should be sought from your midwife or doctor before embarking on any exercise programme.

Mobilisation

Following a Caesarean section, women are encouraged to mobilise early to reduce the risk of deep vein thrombosis. Gone are the days when five to ten days in bed was considered appropriate. If you are up and about within 24 hours of delivery just two to three repetitions of very gentle static abdominal contractions can be performed, then rest. Slowly build up the repetitions to 6–8 in number by 4–6 weeks following delivery. Remember that workload capacity is a very individual thing and should be tailored specifically to each woman's needs.

Resistance work

Generally, after three months postpartum, resistance work or abdominal curls can be introduced. Refer to the beginning of the chapter to remind you of the technique.

Introducing resistance

If the gap between the rectus abdominis muscle is less than two fingers' width, resistance in the form of body weight (lifting head and shoulders from the floor) can be introduced. Follow the instructions for performing abdominal curls as explained at the beginning of this chapter. Remember to watch for 'doming' when lifting head and shoulders which is a sign that the exercise technique may need to be less demanding or technique needs improving. If you cannot maintain a flat abdomen while lifting, continue with pelvic tilting until you can. Perform six to eight repetitions to start, introducing more sets of these as abdominal tone improves.

Increasing abdominal workload

Increase the intensity of the workload by:

1. Introducing half pace lifting. Do this by lifting more slowly into an abdominal curl. This demands good technique and greater strength. Do not be deceived into thinking that a slower 'lift' is easier. Perform one set at half pace, the next set at full pace to the beat of the music if you are using it as a motivator.
2. Increasing the weight to be lifted by folding arms across chest before lifting (see *Figure 6.16a*).
3. Lengthen the lever by placing the fingertips at the side of the head, elbows pointing outward.
4. Introduce abdominal curls with twist (see *Figures 6.17a* and *6.17b*).

Positions for exercising

Lie on back, fingertips behind head, knees bent about 90° and feet hip distance apart.

Technique

Lift head and shoulders, twisting the trunk to the right, touches the left elbow to the right knee as illustrated by *Figure 6.17* and return to starting position. Work each side separately or alternate depending on preference. To progress the exercise further, aim elbow (with fingertips to head) towards opposite knee.

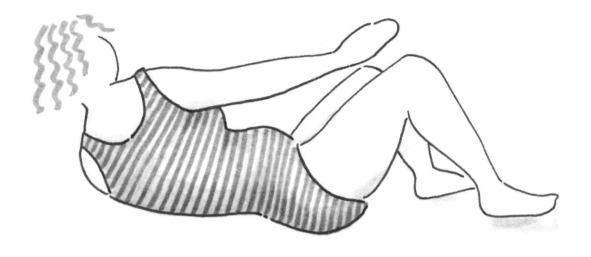

Figure 6.17

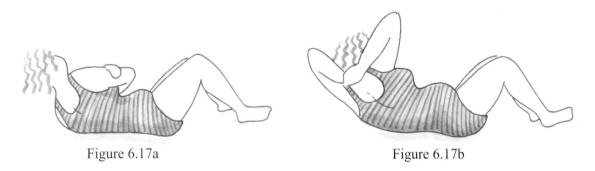

Figure 6.17a   Figure 6.17b

Figure 6.17: Abdominal curl with a twist

Teaching points

- exhale on the lift
- keep elbows out
- do not pull on the head as you lift
- push the small of the back into the floor as you lift
- flatten and tighten the abdomen before lifting
- keep the movement smooth and flowing, do not jerk
- the slower the lift and twist, the harder the exercise
- use half pace to increase intensity of workload.

Rectus abdominis

This muscle is positioned vertically down the front of the abdomen and is in two halves, joining midline. Where these two halves meet (seen externally as a thin brown line running vertically on the abdomen from the umbilicus or navel, down to the symphysis pubis) is the weakened part of the abdominal corset as there is no overlying of other muscle layers but only connective tissue, affected by relaxin hormone. These two halves of rectus muscle are lined and covered by sheaths of fibrous connective tissue from nearby muscles, which unite in the centre. As the abdominal corset stretches to accommodate the growing uterus these two halves of rectus abdominis will commonly separate, caused by a combination of hormonal effect (relaxin), stretching of muscle fibre and excessive strain caused by lengthening of rectus abdominis and the weight of the pregnant uterus falling forward on to the abdominal corset.

Pregnancy implications caused by separation of rectus abdominis (see *Figure 6.18)*

1. Separation of rectus abdominis is common in many women by 26 weeks gestation.
2. Rectus abdominis stretches from 11–12 inches in length to maybe 20 inches (more if it is a multiple pregnancy). The abdominal girth may increase up to 40 inches or more!
3. The abdominal muscles feel deceptively taut as they stretch over the enlarging uterus.
4. Frequent successive pregnancies or multiple pregnancies impose more stress on the abdominal corset and give less chance for improvement in muscle tone. Also, a large baby, excess liquor (water around baby) and obesity will impose extra strain.
5. Performing abdominal curls (lying on the back and lifting head and shoulders off the floor for about a 45° lift) is contraindicated after 16 weeks of pregnancy because of supine hypotensive syndrome. Supine hypotensive syndrome occurs when the pregnant uterus falls backward onto major blood vessels returning blood back to the heart. A reduced amount of blood is pumped back out of the heart, blood pressure begins to drop, the pregnant woman will feel slightly dizzy, may faint if in a prolonged horizontal position on a hard surface. CTG traces (cardiotocography) of babies' heart rates and patterns show that they also feel compromised, even if the woman feels well.

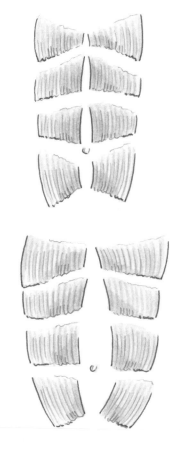

Figure 6.18: Separation of rectus abdominis

6. If abdominal curls are performed throughout pregnancy, the pregnant uterus will be pushed forward against the separating (or separated) rectus abdominis muscle, potentially increasing the gap between the two halves even further.

7. The supportive whole of the abdominal corset that helps to stabilise lumbar regions of the spine is lessened by separation of rectus abdominis.

8. Incorrect alignment of the pelvis with the spine occurs if muscle tone is not maintained, resulting in poor posture, backache and increasing muscle strain. Pelvic tilting will help remedy these problems.

9. Ideally, exercise of the abdominal corset should be commenced as soon as possible so that maximum tone is reached before stretching occurs. Pre-pregnancy tone is ideal.

Postnatal implications of separation of rectus abdominis

1. Reduced support from the abdominal corset for the spine leads to increased backache.

2. All women will have varying degrees of separation of rectus abdominis following delivery of the baby.

3. Type of exercise used will vary from woman to woman, depending on her muscle tone, amount of separation before delivery and size of baby. When to start exercise and when to introduce resistance work (lifting head and shoulders using them as a weight or resistance upon the abdominal corset) will depend entirely on what the gap between the two halves of the rectus abdominis is. It will be different for each individual.

How to check postnatally for separation and amount of gap between the two halves of the rectus abdominis muscle

Position

Lie flat on back, knees bent, feet flat on floor.

Technique

Breathe in, pull in abdominal muscles and try to flatten abdomen, maintaining a flat stomach. Reach with right hand across to touch the left knee. Before you reach across to touch the opposite knee place two fingers longitudinally just below your navel and try to feel for a gap between the two halves of muscle as you lift head and shoulders. How many fingers can you insert lengthways? A bulge in the centre area when performing abdominal curls will also confirm separation. Two fingers' or more gap contraindicates any resistance work or abdominal curls. Simple pelvic tilting, on a firm surface, should begin as soon as possible after delivery, to gently counteract the 'baggy stretched muscle syndrome'.

Postnatal variations

Do not consider other exercises for the abdominal corset, eg. twisting or bending to the side until the gap between the rectus abdominis has closed. Indirectly other muscles (internal and external oblique and transverse abdominis) are attached to the rectus abdominis and potential muscle imbalance may create tension on the two halves of the rectus abdominis again.

Pelvic floor

What is it?

A sling of muscle attached to the pelvic bone at the front, passing in two halves to the sacrum and coccyx at the back of the pelvis. The two halves fan out to form the 'floor' of the pelvis. Three openings pass through this hammock or sling of muscle, the urethra, the vagina, and the rectum.

Role of pelvic floor

To support abdominal contents, to control leakage of urine. Stress incontinence occurs if muscles of the pelvic floor lose tone and the reflex tightening of the sphincters around the vagina, urethra and rectum is slowed down due to poor muscle action. If good tone is present then the fast 'twitch' muscle fibres react quickly to 'close up' urethra and rectum.

Pelvic floor muscles

It is made up of two layers — a deep layer of muscle and a superficial layer of muscle.

Deep muscle layer: the levator ani muscles in two halves consist of the ilio-coccygeus, ischio-coccygeus and the pubo-coccygeus. These react very quickly to changes in intra-abdominal pressure, eg. coughing, vomiting, sneezing, defecation. These are made of 'fast twitch' muscle fibres that produce a reflex action for quick contraction of short duration (see *Figure 6.19*).

Superficial muscle layer: transverse perineum, bulbo-cavernous, ischio-cavernous.

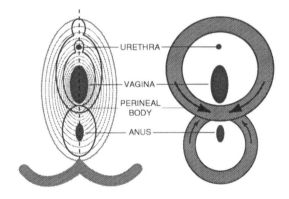

Figure 6.19: The pelvic floor

Obstetric factors affecting pelvic floor function:

* Previous third degree tear or slow healing.
* Breakdown of perineum.
* Instrumental delivery last time (extra stress).
* Prolonged stress incontinence last time.
* Grande multips or multiple pregnancy.
* 60% primiparae experience stress incontinence for first time during pregnancy.
* Little difference in increase in severity until parity reaches four or more.
* Many women spontaneously resolve in the first six weeks postpartum — an important minority persist.
* In a study of 1000 mothers 19% had stress incontinence at three months postpartum.

Issues of debate

* Is perineal trauma at delivery an aggravating factor?

* Do liberal use of episiotomies prevent trauma? Research suggests not.

* It is believed that women who have had a prolonged second stage labour, forceps deliveries and large babies (over 4 kgs) are particularly at risk of developing incontinence, though more statistical evidence is needed (Henry *et al*, 1982).

Problems of exercising the pelvic floor

* It is difficult to know if the exercise is being performed correctly.

* Inserting a finger into the vagina while tightening the pelvic floor muscles is used by some as a method of assessing pelvic floor function. This is not acceptable to some women.

* Difficult in early postpartum days or weeks for some women. Soreness, bruised and swollen perineum prevent effective pelvic floor contractions.

A very large study was held in 1985–87 (Sleep and Grant) in West Berkshire Hospital on 1,800 women. Conventional ante- and postnatal pelvic floor exercises were evaluated in two groups: one had intensive continuing educational and clinical support for three months and one group did not. The results did not support the hypothesis about the value and content of exercises offered to women around childbirth.

Exercising the pelvic floor

Positions for this exercise

Almost any position you can think of, standing, sitting (with knees apart), lying with both knees bent or sitting in a chair.

Exercise technique

Tighten the ring of muscle around the back passage, tighten the ring of muscle around the entrance to the vagina, pull up inside (imagine stopping the flow of urine) hold for four to six seconds then release.

It is important that you do not:

* Hold your breath! Instead, once you have tightened your pelvic floor take a slow deep breath in, breathe out, then release the pelvic floor muscles.

* Over-tighten the abdominal muscles and buttock muscles at the same time as exercising the pelvic floor. Some tightening is inevitable, but do not substitute those muscles for your pelvic floor.

* Think that holding the contraction of your pelvic floor for much longer than six seconds will make it stronger or faster; it will not. Pelvic floor muscles are made up of fast twitch muscle fibres; this means that they work best for short periods of contraction. Slow twitch muscle fibres also contract to fulfil the 'supportive sling' function of the pelvic floor.

* Squeeze the legs together and tense the inner thigh muscles. The pelvic floor muscles are not attached in any way to the tops of the thighbone, so squeezing the legs together does not help

in any way. For this reason, when sitting knees should be apart when 'pulling up' your pelvic floor.

* Worry that certain positions such as 'tailor' sitting, sitting with the soles of feet together, squatting or sitting with your knees pulled up and apart will stretch your pelvic floor — they will not. They do, however, stretch the inner thigh muscles and increased flexibility in this area may make the second stage of labour position more comfortable for you.

Stress incontinence

This includes:
- an involuntary loss of urine
- wetting yourself as a result of physical exertion
- stress incontinence being a 'symptom' not the cause
- it is nothing to do with mental or emotional problems.

Some common causes of stress incontinence are:
- coughing and sneezing
- running and athletic activities
- impact aerobics
- laughing.

In more severe cases stress incontinence can occur when:
- walking
- getting up from a chair
- turning over in bed.

It is often a hidden problem of pregnancy with some excuses for stress incontinence being:
- is it the price of childbearing?
- I have always had a weak bladder
- it's just a woman's problem
- what can you expect at my age?
- it's not important enough to bother the doctor with
- it's socially embarrassing to talk about the genital area.

You should consult your doctor if:
- you have blood in your urine
- it is painful when you empty your bladder
- you need to empty your bladder straight away, having just been
- you have difficulty in starting to urinate or a slow stream when you have started
- you experience continual 'dribbling'
- your problem appeared after a long period of healthy bladder control
- your problem is creating stress and possibly interfering with your normal lifestyle.

Muscular strengthen and endurance teaching aid

Muscle Groups	Pectorals	Trapezius	Triceps	Gluteals	Hamstrings	Quadruceps	Abductors	Gastrocnemius
Exercises	Pecdecs	Shoulder squeezes	Triceps kick back	Back leg raises	Hamstring curls	Half squats	Side leg raises	Single/double heel raises
Teaching position	Seated or standing	Seated or standing	Seated or standing	Standing with support	Standing with support	Standing	Lie on side or standing	Seated or standing
Teaching points	Do not drop elbows during work. Do not fling the arms back on return	Make the action smooth. Draw elbows down and back. Relax on the reach forward.	Keep upper arm tucked into side of body. Do not move the upper arm. Keep shoulders relaxed	Ensure support. Swing leg back supporting it with a soft knee. Keep leg straight as if it is lifted straight behind. Do not lift leg too high	Support leg with soft knee. As foot is lifted up toward the bottom squeeze the muscles to enhance the exercise. Keep movement smooth	Feet slightly wider than hips and pointing on the diagonal. Bend knees and stick bottom out. As squat occurs keep knees in line with ankles	Ensure support by keeping the knees soft. Do not turn knee out as leg is lifted to the side. Do not lift leg too high. If any pain occurs in SP area stop the exercise. Use hand on the floor for support if lying down	Use wall or chair for support. Do not turn feet over as heels are lifted. Do not rock the toes off the floor on descent
1st trimester	Can use box position for press ups	Do 6–8 reps more if able	Do tricep dips seated on the floor using body weight as resistance	As pre-pregnancy regime	6–8 reps with 2–3 sets if regular exerciser	Free standing. 12+reps, 2–3 sets if regular exerciser, less if not	At pre-pregnancy level. Do not lift leg too high due to relaxin effect	Joints will be effected by relaxin especially if overweight. Monitor technique
2nd trimester	Wall press up or box position for press ups	Decrease reps and sets	Perform standing or in a pool using water as resistance	Do not hollow back due to frontload weight	Provide support. Reduce reps to 6–8 reps	Ensure support bar is available. Reduce reps and sets	Provide support bar. Reduce reps to 6–8 reps	Provide a support bar. Reduce reps and sets
3rd trimester	Seated on a chair or standing against pool wall. Box position with careful attention to a straight back	Rest and rotation of other muscle groups in between exercises. Consider seating	Keep to 6–8 reps. If tired use hand paddles if a regular exerciser, in water based class	If tired do as many as able. For regular exercises do 2 sets each side.	Provide chairs, bars or walls for support. Reduce reps as required	More reps allowed if performed in an aquanatal class as supported by water. If tired reduce reps and sets	Lie on side to exercise. 6–8 reps each side for 2 sets will be adequate for most.	If prone to cramp reduce reps and sets. Ensure support bar available. More reps in pool as gravity is removed. Sit for exercise

7

Aquanatal classes

'Aquanatal' is a form of exercise specially designed for the pregnant woman, that includes dance-like movements starting with a 'warm-up' section, it is then interspersed with cardiovascular work, muscular strength and endurance exercises and ending with a 'cool-down' section, stretch and relaxation exercises. They are all performed to music with the individual in chest-deep water. The structural programme takes into account the limitations and physiological changes of pregnancy.

Properties of immersion in water

Buoyancy

Gravity pulls body down → Pressure of water increases → Creates upward lift on body = Buoyancy

Density of the body

Buoyancy is determined by density of body. Almost total immersion is needed before the individual can floating easily. Position or 'fatty tissue' on the body determines how easy it is to float.

Gravity effects in water

Immersion in neck deep water reduces the effects of gravity by up to 90% and thereby reduces the compression stress on weight bearing joints, bones and muscles. In waist deep water the reduction is 50%. Exercise in water facilitates a greater range of movement in the joints, enhancing mobility.

Support

Water provides good support for those who are less confident. It is important to consider supporting positions for stretch and MSE work in a water based environment.

Knowledge base required by the professional

In terms of exercises in water, as an instructor it will be important to know the following:
- the physiological effects of immersion in water
- the structure of a fitness class
- the advantages of exercising in water

- body mechanics, for instance how the body works during movement and exercise, eg. kinesiology and how this changes in a water environment
- physiological changes of pregnancy relating to exercise limitations
- contraindicated exercises
- the importance of screening procedures
- how to choreograph routines
- music in terms of how to select suitable pieces of music and how to break it down
- muscle groups, how they work, what action they perform, teaching position, technique, corrections and alternative positions.

Advantages of exercising in water

Water is an alternative medium for the pregnant woman to exercise in and thereby receive advice on health and fitness. It offers the following potential benefits:

- less stress on joints
- exercise is possible for individuals with limited mobility
- water-based exercise is good for rehabilitation
- the hydrostatic force of water, extra buoyancy and improved thermoregulation give advantages to the pregnant woman over land-based exercise
- the haemodynamic changes of pregnancy, affected by immersion, may put less strain on the uterine blood flow than land-based exercise
- water is 'environmentally friendly', giving less risk of injury generally
- the resistance factor of water enhances the effect of the exercise
- chronic backache is often relieved, as the weight of the uterus and its contents is temporarily removed during immersion
- women feel lighter and more graceful, leading to improved self-esteem
- Certain exercises are more easy to perform due to the support of water, eg. press-ups against the pool side.

Physiological effects of immersion in chest-deep water

The hydrostatic pressure of water exerts a force proportional to the depth of immersion. This pressure acts uniformly throughout the body. Extravascular fluid is pushed into the vascular space, resulting in rapid expansion of plasma volume. The greater the amount of extravascular fluid, the more plasma is transferred. Central blood volume is expanded due to the outside pressure of water on the body. The expansion of plasma volume bypasses the lymphatic system. This effect is less at night than during the day. All of these changes occur within seconds of immersion.

Immersion of the pregnant woman for 20–40 minutes results in 300–400 ml loss in fluid, while blood volume is maintained. Renal vascular resistance decreases which results in an increased blood flow through the kidney and an increased filtration rate. Urate excretion increases and reabsorption of sodium decreases. This diuretic effect peaks within one hour, and within four hours the urine flow returns to normal. Therefore, fluid retention in the pregnant woman may be relieved by immersion of water.

Cardiac output and stroke volume are increased and heart rate, blood pressure and oedema are decreased. Fetal heart rate and uterine tone are unchanged. Maternal heart rate during water-based exercise is lower than during land-based exercise. A final thought on this is that aquanatal exercise could offer a new way of treating hypertensive disease in pregnancy.

SOS — safety, observation and screening

The instructor of the aquanatal session, who should be observing, demonstrating and teaching the session from the pool side needs to wear flat, rubber-bottomed shoes or trainers. Appropriate safe footwear is a must due to the wet and slippery poolside environment. If a very warm hydrotherapy pool is used, the instructor may prefer to wear a swimsuit, as bodyline and exercise technique can easily be observed by the participants of the class. This also ensures that the instructor's own body temperature does not become uncomfortably high. A loose tracksuit and T-shirt may be preferred by some, but should not be so baggy that they obliterate visually the technique of some exercises which may compromise the safety of the class. A pool side attendant should be on duty at all times while the class is in progress. The attendant, usually provided by the fitness centre, should be well-versed in the techniques of lifesaving and safety standards. Any electrical equipment used on the pool side should be plugged into the mains via a special adapter called a 'contact-breaker', available from major stores at a cost of around £15. This deals immediately with any electrical dysfunction by breaking from the mains supply, thus enhancing the safety of the operator.

All participants must be screened first. Questions that should be asked include:

* Any problems with past or present pregnancy?
* Any medical problems, eg. asthma, epilepsy, diabetes?
* Any joint, muscle or bone injuries; any back problems?
* Any medicines being taken at present?

If the answer is 'yes' to any question then a detailed history should be taken and advice given as to whether to take part or not. Adaptations of the class to suit the individual is also a possibility (see *Chapter 5*, Screening and safety aspects).

Water temperature

Hydrotherapy pools offer an ideal environment, with temperatures often of 89–91°F (32–33°C). In practice, I find that water temperature below 87°F (30°C) is too uncomfortable as 'cooling off' occurs rapidly which negates the effect of the 'warm-up' and leaves mothers feeling cool, uncomfortable and certainly not willing to relax at the end of the session. As the pregnant woman's body is generally half a degree warmer than her non-pregnant equivalent, the effects of cooler water are felt more keenly. Classes can be conducted in water temperatures of 87–89°F (30–32°C) but the structure and content of the components must reflect the environment. Therefore, the class needs to include more pulse-raising activities throughout the session, not just during the warm-up section. This is to ensure that the inner core temperature of the body and muscles is maintained, preventing the inherent risk of injury that cold muscles are more susceptible to.

Availability of sessions

Ideally, a private session, separate from the general public, booked just for the aquanatal class, gives pregnant women the chance to relax more easily. There is also less danger of being kicked, splashed or jumped on, and the opportunity for private conversation with the tutor. If this is not available then the pool will 'rope off' two or three lanes of water, so that the class may be conducted while another class, such as an 'aquatots' session with mothers, is undertaken in the other part of the pool.

The class structure

The water-based session should be structured in the same way as any normal land-based exercise class. It should consist of the following sections.

Warm-up exercises

This section begins to mobilise the body as well as warm-up muscles and joints. It includes:

- mobility of major joints
- 'moving' or pulse raising steps designed to gently increase the pulse
- static stretches: these should then be performed to complete the warm-up session, to ease out the muscles, preparing the body for the work to follow.

See *Chapter 4* for a detailed explanation of the warm-up process and the structure of a fitness class.

Stamina section or cardiovascular work

This can be achieved by swimming, walking briskly through the water, kicking legs or using arms and floats. Participants should be encouraged to work out at their own level, 15–20 minutes if a regular exerciser or proficient swimmer. When necessary, the pregnant woman should bring her workload down by walking through the water, then commencing pulse raising work again when she feels ready to. Class members should be encouraged to talk to each other during this part of the class, as uncomfortably breathless conversation is a sign that the woman is working at a level that would be detrimental to the fetus or baby, ie. a maternal pulse above 140 beats per minute. Choreographed exercise routines, using large muscle groups and resistance of water (half squats, marching, side steps) using the motivation of music are great fun and can enhance the aerobic section of the class.

Many pregnant women adopt breaststroke when swimming. Providing there is no discomfort over and around the symphysis pubis joint when performing the leg kick, then this type of stroke is perfectly acceptable. Obviously, if discomfort occurs this type of leg kick should be discouraged. At the end of this session the instructor brings the workload down gradually by 'walking' everyone through the water for one or two widths.

Muscular strength and endurance exercises.

Different muscle groups are exercised, with care taken to rotate areas of the body worked, so that repetitions are not excessive. The ideal is only six to eight repetitions per muscle group worked, as pregnant women tire easily. The supportive nature of the environment enhances body positions and extra work from the muscle group can be achieved more safely and with greater ease using the resistance factor of the water.

Cool-down and relaxation

This section should follow the 'work' of the session. Static held stretches should be employed to gently ease out the muscles that have just been worked. When stretching, the minimum pressure to achieve a mild feeling of tension should be employed, as relaxin hormone, produced by the corpus luteum and reaching its maximum level at 12 weeks gestation, softens ligaments that support joints, and an overstretched ligament will result in a more unstable joint as discussed earlier in this book. The stretch should be held for about 8–10 second. It should be sustained, static and never bounced, as this will stimulate the muscle to stay tight, and relaxation and lengthening of the muscle to its pre-exercise length will not occur.

The relaxation session at the end of the class can be enhanced by offering a variety of floating aids including:

- inflatable neck floats
- large tyres
- various-sized polystyrene floats.

As with other sections of the class, appropriate music can help to create the right atmosphere.

The National Perspective — some concerns

Aquanatal exercise is a service that is being increasingly offered to the pregnant woman by a wide range of individuals and professionals — some trained, some not. The popularity and uptake of the service, not only by mothers but also by midwives and other interested parties, can be viewed as positive in so far as a structured, well-taught session offered by appropriately trained instructors does much to introduce, initiate and enhance the principles of health-related fitness. However, despite the fact that the development of aquanatal and exercise to music classes embraces the concept of the government report *A Healthy Nation*, there are some issues that need to be examined.

Many conversations and communications with midwives both nationally and internationally have shown a wide variation in how this service is being offered. A number of midwives are voicing concern that this service is being taught by unqualified, non-professional, untrained exercise and swimming teachers in a variety of situations, for example at leisure and fitness centres. Pregnant women are being allowed to continue with their 'usual' high-energy, high-input exercise sessions, with comments like, *You'll be OK — I'll keep an eye on you*. Not reassuring, in fact, as there is no general knowledge of the very special considerations necessary to make an exercise session for the pregnant woman beneficial and safe. Some leisure centres have even actively refused midwifery involvement and advice in their sessions

Midwifery managers in some areas are not supporting their staff who are interested in offering this invaluable and important part of their clinical and educational role, which directly affects maternal self-esteem and motivates further involvement in the uptake of a service that will benefit mothers and babies. Midwives should be supported and actively encouraged to attend an approved course of instruction that will make them more competent in this area of expertise. Physical education is the grassroots of health education in its widest form and it seems incredible that some midwives and managers feel that teaching or supervising antenatal exercise to music, in whatever medium, is not really midwifery. The health and education of the pregnant woman are paramount for the midwife who offers the service.

In order to control, monitor and develop the field of exercise during pregnancy some guidelines are needed. Consideration should be given to:

- training methods
- scrutinisation of and decisions on acceptable 'bodies' of expertise
- the feasibility of standardising course content
- the discussion on who should teach pregnant women to exercise
- the introduction of health-related fitness principles to modules of midwifery training as a baseline of knowledge to be expanded further if directed at post-basic level.

There are many different courses available to train midwives and professionals, offering a diversity of training methods and levels of suitability. A working party should be established to set the expected aims and objectives, and to establish uniformly acceptable baselines of knowledge that professionals should achieve in order to teach pregnant women.

Interest and motivation in this field of expertise is rising fast. It should be harnessed and moulded into an extension of a service that we can be proud of. It is important that this quality of service is ensured in the future.

8

Some guidelines on exercise activities

Step classes

As most step classes are longer than 15–20 minutes, aerobic work in this environment may be limited for pregnant women. The length of class and intensity of the workload may precipitate overheating and dehydration. Also, complex choreography on and off the step may be too demanding for a pregnant woman who is more clumsy, much heavier and lacking in coordination especially if a beginner at exercising. If the step is lowered right down and used in a specifically designed pregnancy fitness class then an experienced instructor may use this form of aerobic work as part of her class. Special attention to technique is vital to avoid impact problems of joints, back and pelvic floor. Steps used in the swimming pool present less of a safety problem and can add variety to an aquanatal class.

Contact sports

Contact sports, such as hockey and netball, present particular problems, as any contact at speed with another participant can result in potential injury to the mother or baby by direct physical trauma. The pace and agility needed naturally screen out participation by most pregnant women. Diving and horse riding should be avoided. It is not the actual horse riding that presents the danger but the potential to falloff or be thrown off that eliminates participation.

Cycling

Lack of balance, coordination and the danger of falling off can present problems after the first trimester of pregnancy. A static cycle at home or in the gym will be safer as pregnancy progresses. Be aware of how long and what level pulse to work out at, for example, above 15–20 minutes work with a pulse rate no higher than 140 beats per minute.

Weight training

Continue only with light (2lb) hand-held weights to maintain some muscle tone. The potential Valsalva effect when breath holding and lifting weights can raise blood pressure and the weights can detrimentally affect relaxin induced unstable joints. Do not embark on using weights for the first time once pregnant.

Running and jogging

Pregnancy is not the time to take up running and jogging for the first time. Experienced runners and joggers should bring their workload down to two miles or less a day. Research suggests that most experienced joggers are covering a mile and a half a day or less by the third trimester. Again heat production, dehydration and vulnerable joints affected by relaxin hormone are the major considerations.

Swimming

Swimming is an ideal exercise for the pregnant woman. If a non-swimmer, wading through chest-deep water and participating in aquanatal classes will give great benefits. The breaststroke leg kick may give discomfort around the symphysis pubis joint at the front of the pelvis. If so, use the front crawl leg kick instead. Read *Chapter 7* for a more detailed examination of exercise classes in water.

Walking

This is an excellent form of exercise and all pregnant women should be able to participate in this activity, regardless of their personal circumstances. Pushing toddlers in prams up and down can be an easy way of maintaining cardiac fitness. Speed walking can be utilised instead of running and jogging. Supportive footwear is essential as the extra weight of pregnancy throws more demands on to ankle joints and the arches of the foot and the joints will be affected by relaxin hormone. Physiological oedema of the ankles may be reduced by walking as circulation is enhanced.

9

Some postnatal considerations

Following delivery, the uterus or womb involutes (or shrinks) back down to its pre-pregnant state by six weeks postpartum. It is usually not palpable abdominally by 10–12 days following delivery. A vaginal discharge of a watery blood stained, mucous nature gradually diminishes and by three weeks after delivery has usually ceased. The abdominal wall feels lax and soft for some weeks to come. Changes that had taken place in the urinary system take at least eight weeks to reverse and most pregnancy hormone levels have reverted to their pre-pregnancy levels by about thirty days postpartum with the exception of relaxin hormone. Perineal sutures should have healed within 7–14 days following delivery, although some women experience difficulty and healing may be slower than normal. Even so, most perineums should be completely healed by six weeks postpartum.

How a woman reacts and recovers from the birth process is, naturally, a very individual thing, and because of this all embracing statements of when one should start to exercise again cannot be used. Factors that will affect a woman's capacity to return to regular exercise will include postnatal checks and are usually carried out at about six to eight weeks. After this time most women should be able to exercise regularly again.

When to exercise and type of delivery

Sore perineums, forceps delivery, Ventouse extractions and Caesarean sectin prohibit commencement of exercise. The opportunity to allow the body to rest and recover for a few week is vital. Do not rush if sore, exhausted and lacking in sleep. Take things more steadily.

Haemoglobin status

If blood loss at delivery was more than normal, or a low haemoglobin level was present before delivery, aerobic capacity can be enormously affected, resulting in breathlessness on just walking or climbing stairs. Wait until haemoglobin levels are within a normal range before exercising again. Iron therapy from the GP should resolve this for most women and it will take three to four months before a level of 12–14g/dl is reached.

Pelvic floor problems

Most perineums should be healed within two weeks of delivery. Some women experience long term problems, such as stress incontinence, scar tissue, discomfort and problems in resuming sexual intercourse. Specialist advice should be sought immediately and before embarking on any exercise programme. As relaxin hormone will still influence soft supportive tissues and ligaments, the structure of a postnatal class should reflect this by ensuring that there is little or no impact movement in the postnatal class for three to five months. Pelvic floor exercises should be recommenced as soon as possible following delivery. In my practical experience, it is not unusual for it to take 9–12 months before a woman can re-engage in high energy impact classes without suffering from stress incontinence. See *Chapter 6*, for more information about the pelvic floor.

Backache

The backache of pregnancy does not necessarily disappear overnight with the arrival of the baby. Although previous biomechanical issues may have suddenly disappeared, other problems may take their place. If an epidural was used as a form of pain relief, inappropriate body position during labour may not have been noticed until the epidural wore off. Backache may result. Also, breast feeding without appropriate support, or incorrect technique will produce backache. Bending and lifting will form a large part of a mother's day, now that the baby has arrived. Incorrect technique will produce more backache. Avoid heavy weight lifting for at least 12 weeks. Because of the potential for more or increased backache, special attention should be paid to posture and promoting correct technique of back strengthening exercises, and abdominal exercises that will help support the back.

Symphysis pubis joint — subluxation

Some women are unfortunate enough to experience subluxation of the symphysis pubis joint during pregnancy, or in the postnatal period. This can result in being confined to a wheelchair, if severe, or having to use a walking stick, alongside specialist advice and treatment from physiotherapists. Obviously most exercise for this group of women is extremely limited, although the upper body can be mobilised, warmed up and exercised in a seated position.

Sacro-iliac joint discomfort

These two very powerful joints, situated on the back of the pelvis, are affected by relaxin hormone and a small range of movement naturally occurs here during pregnancy. Very large babies may produce more stress on these joints and the effects of relaxin postnatally may give rise to discomfort and an unstable pelvic girdle, especially if the symphysis pubis joint is also affected; special consideration must be given to weight bearing exercise and strength work to ensure totally supported body positions, or no exercise regimes until the effects of the delivery have totally abated.

Separation of rectus abdominis

This has been discussed in some detail in *Chapter 6.* Postnatal implications and checking for separation of rectus abdominis are illustrated and also a gradual return to resistance work for the abdominal corset and oblique work (lifting and twisting to the right or left). Strong resistance work should be discouraged until the gap between the two halves of the rectus abdominis has decreased. In the meantime use static abdominal contractions, pelvic tilting and correct posture.Do not rush back to abdominal work too soon. Patience and appropriate exercise with good technique for a few months will pay many dividends later. Remember it took almost a childbearing year for those pregnancy changes to affect your body this way. They will not reverse overnight.

Caesarean section delivery

Women should have their postnatal check and ensure that the section scar has healed before taking part in exercise programmes again. Any scar tenderness or discharge should be reported to your midwife or doctor immediately. Most sections scars are healed externally by two to three weeks postpartum with alternate or bead sutures removed at six days post delivery. Specifically designed postnatal exercise classes would be appropriate from six weeks of delivery.

Breast feeding

Some research suggests that regular exercisers have raised prolactin levels, a bonus for breast feeders. A well supporting bra should be worn at all times and especially when exercising postnatally. Some exercises may be uncomfortable to perform if breasts are lactating and a feed is due, for instance pec deck or back extensions from a flat lying position. Adapt your programme accordingly.

Tiredness

Most newly delivered women feel exhausted in those first few weeks. Not only does the body have to adapt to the birth process and the ensuing reversion physiologically of all systems, new mothers have to come to terms with their role of being a mother and all the responsibility this entails. The baby will be playing havoc with most sleep routines and most parents feel very tired for a few months. Once the baby has settled into a feeding routine and a sleep pattern that allows you regular sleep, exercise classes can be started again. Do not participate if you are feeling exhausted as you will be more prone to injury.

Weight gain

After the postnatal check many women are between 14–20lbs heavier than before pregnancy. Obviously, cardiovascular, or aerobic work will help to burn up those unwanted pounds and specialist advice may need to be given on diet, particularly if breast feeding. Dieting is to be discouraged. Walking briskly and swimming are excellent forms of exercise for the recently delivered mother who wants to start an exercise programme before her postnatal check.

References and further reading

Henry MM, Parks AG, Swash M (1982) The pelvic floor musculature in the descending pereneum syndrome. *Br J Surg* **69**: 470–2

Knuttgen HG, Kendall E (1974) Physiological response to pregnancy at restand during exercise. *J Applied Physio* **3**: 549–552

Lotgering FK, Gilbert RD, Longo LD (1986) Maternal and fetal responses to exercise during pregnancy. *Physiological Reviews. The American Physiological Society* **65**(1): 1–36

Mittlemark R, Wisewell R, Drinkwater B (1991) *Exercise in Pregnancy.* 2nd edn. Williams & Wilkins, Baltimore, Maryland

Noble E (1985) *Essential Exercises for The Childbearing Year.* 2nd edn. John Murray Ltd, London

Wallace AM, Boyner DB, Dan A (1986) Aerobic exercise, maternal self-esteem and physical discomfort during pregnancy. *J Nurse-Midwifery* **31**(6): 255–262

Whiteford B, Polden M (1988) *Postnatal Exercises.* Century Publishing, London

White J (1992) Exercising for two — what's safe for the active pregnant woman? *The Physician and Sports Medicine,* **20**(5): 179–182

Thompson CW, Floyd RT (1994) *Manual of Structural Kinesiology.* 12th edn. Mosby Publishing, St Louis, USA

Further reading

American College of Obstetricians and Gynaecology (1994) ACOG issues, recommendations on exercising during pregnancy and the postpartum period. *Am Family Physician* **49**(5): 1258–1259

Anderson B (1998) *Stretching.* Pelham Books, London

Association of Chartered Physiotherapists in Obstetrics and Gynaecology (1990) *Care of your body in pregnancy.* ACPOG, London

Baddeley S, Green S (1991) Are midwives fit to teach? *Mod Midwife* **1**(3):14–15

Baddeley S (1991) Health-related fitness during pregnancy. *Mod Midwife* **1**(3):16–17

Baddeley S (1993) Aquanatal classes. *Mod Midwife* July/August: 16–18

Bell R, O'Neill M (1994) Exercise and Pregnancy: A review. *Birth* **21**: 85–95

Bell R, Palma SM, Lumley JM (1995) The effect of vigorous exercise during pregnancy on birth weight. *Aust N Z J Obstet Gynaecol* **35**(part 1): 46–51

Calguneri M, Bird HA, Wright V (1982) Changes in joint laxity during pregnancy. *Annals of the Rheumatic Disease* **41**: 126–28

Clapp JF (1994) A clinical approach to exercising during pregnancy. *Clinics in Sports Medicine* **13**(2): 443–455

Clapp JF (1991) The changing thermal response to endurance exercise during pregnancy. *Am J Obstets Gynecol* **165**(6): 1684–1689

Degani S, Lewinsky R, Shapiro I (1989) Maternal exercise test in the assessment of fetal arrhythmia. *J Obstet Gynaecol* **9**(4): 277–280

Fishbein E, Phillips M (1990) How safe is exercise during pregnancy? *J Obs Gynae Neonatal Nurs* **19**(1): 45–8

Hale RW (1987) Exercise and pregnancy. How each affects the other. *Postgrad Med* **82**(3): 61–63

Lumley J, Astbury J (1989) Advice for pregnancy. In: Chalmers I, Enkin M, Keirse MJNC (eds) *Effective care in pregnancy and childbirth*. Vol 1. Oxford University Press, Oxford: 237–254

Marshall VA (1991) Maternal health practices and complications of term labour. *J Nurse Midwifery* **36**(3): 168–173

Moore K, Dumas GA, Reid JG *et al* (1988) *A longitudinal study of the mechanical changes in posture associated with pregnancy. A preliminary report.* Proceedings taken from the Fifth Biennial Conference and Symposium: 114–115

Morton MJ, Paul MS, Campos GR *et al* (1985) Exercise dynamics in late gestation: effects of physical training. *Am J Obstet Gynecol* **152**(1): 91–97

Mowbray C (1998) *YMCA Guide to Exercise to Music.* Pelham Books, London

Pivarnik JM, James M (1994) Maternal exercise during pregnancy. *Sports Medicine* **18**(4): 215–217

Pivarnik JM, Lee W, Clark SL *et al* (1990) Cardiac output responses of primigravid women during exercise determined by the direct Fick technique. *Obs Gynecol* **75**(6): 954–959

Seanae Y (1993) Exercise guidelines for pregnant women. *J of Nurs Scholarship* **26**(4): 265–269

Shepherd RJ (1994) *Aerobic fitness and health.* Human Kinetics Publishers: chap 5

Smith M, Upfold J, Edwards M (1988) The dangers of heat to the unborn. *Patient Management* **17**(3): 157–165

South-Paul JE, Rajagopal KR, Tenholder MF (1988) The effect of participation in a regular exercise program upon aerobic capacity during pregnancy. *Obs Gynecol* **71**(2): 175–179

Watson WJ, Katz VL, Hackney AC *et al* (1991) Fetal responses to maximal swimming and cycling exercise during pregnancy. *Obstet Gynecol* **77**(3): 382–386

Wirhead R (1989) *Athletic Ability and the Anatomy of Motion.* Wolfe Medical Publications Ltd, London

Williams A, Rafla N, Campbell I *et al* (1988) Keep fit in pregnancy. *Nurs Times* **84**(29): 54

Wolfe LA, Mothola MF (1993) Aerobic exercise in pregnancy: an update. *Can J Appl Physiol* **18**(2): 119–147

Index